OPPOSING
VIEWPOINTS®
SERIES

D0839814

Domestic Terrorism

Other Books of Related Interest

Opposing Viewpoints Series

Hacking and Freedom of Information
Immigration Bans
Violent Video Games and Society
Western Democracy at Risk

At Issue Series

Cyberwarfare
Domestic Terrorism
The Ethics of WikiLeaks
Guns: Conceal and Carry

Current Controversies Series

Antifa and the Radical Left
The Dark Web
Political Extremism in the United States
Whistleblowers

> "Congress shall make no law … abridging the freedom of speech, or of the press."

First Amendment to the US Constitution

The basic foundation of our democracy is the First Amendment guarantee of freedom of expression. The Opposing Viewpoints series is dedicated to the concept of this basic freedom and the idea that it is more important to practice it than to enshrine it.

OPPOSING
VIEWPOINTS®
SERIES

| Domestic Terrorism

Gary Wiener, Book Editor

GREENHAVEN
PUBLISHING

Published in 2021 by Greenhaven Publishing, LLC
353 3rd Avenue, Suite 255, New York, NY 10010

First Edition

Articles in Greenhaven Publishing anthologies are often edited for length to meet page
requirements. In addition, original titles of these works are changed to clearly present
the main thesis and to explicitly indicate the author's opinion. Every effort is made to
ensure that Greenhaven Publishing accurately reflects the original intent of the authors.
Every effort has been made to trace the owners of the copyrighted material.

Cover image: Boston Globe/Getty Images

Library of Congress Cataloging-in-Publication Data

Names: Wiener, Gary, editor.
Title: Domestic terrorism / Gary Wiener, book editor.
Description: New York : Greenhaven Publishing, 2021. | Series: Opposing
    viewpoints | Includes bibliographical references and index. | Audience: Grades 9–12.
Identifiers: LCCN 2020000592 | ISBN 9781534506954 (library binding) | ISBN
    9781534506947 (paperback)
Subjects: LCSH: Domestic terrorism—United States—Juvenile literature. |
    Terrorists—United States—Juvenile literature. | Domestic
    terrorism—United States—Prevention.
Classification: LCC HV6432 .D664 2020 | DDC 363.3250973—dc23
LC record available at https://lccn.loc.gov/2020000592

Manufactured in the United States of America

Website: http://greenhavenpublishing.com

Contents

The Importance of Opposing Viewpoints

Perhaps every generation experiences a period in time in which the populace seems especially polarized, starkly divided on the important issues of the day and gravitating toward the far ends of the political spectrum and away from a consensus-facilitating middle ground. The world that today's students are growing up in and that they will soon enter into as active and engaged citizens is deeply fragmented in just this way. Issues relating to terrorism, immigration, women's rights, minority rights, race relations, health care, taxation, wealth and poverty, the environment, policing, military intervention, the proper role of government—in some ways, perennial issues that are freshly and uniquely urgent and vital with each new generation—are currently roiling the world.

If we are to foster a knowledgeable, responsible, active, and engaged citizenry among today's youth, we must provide them with the intellectual, interpretive, and critical-thinking tools and experience necessary to make sense of the world around them and of the all-important debates and arguments that inform it. After all, the outcome of these debates will in large measure determine the future course, prospects, and outcomes of the world and its peoples, particularly its youth. If they are to become successful members of society and productive and informed citizens, students need to learn how to evaluate the strengths and weaknesses of someone else's arguments, how to sift fact from opinion and fallacy, and how to test the relative merits and validity of their own opinions against the known facts and the best possible available information. The landmark series Opposing Viewpoints has been providing students with just such critical-thinking skills and exposure to the debates surrounding society's most urgent contemporary issues for many years, and it continues to serve this essential role with undiminished commitment, care, and rigor.

The key to the series's success in achieving its goal of sharpening students' critical-thinking and analytic skills resides in its title—

Opposing Viewpoints. In every intriguing, compelling, and engaging volume of this series, readers are presented with the widest possible spectrum of distinct viewpoints, expert opinions, and informed argumentation and commentary, supplied by some of today's leading academics, thinkers, analysts, politicians, policy makers, economists, activists, change agents, and advocates. Every opinion and argument anthologized here is presented objectively and accorded respect. There is no editorializing in any introductory text or in the arrangement and order of the pieces. No piece is included as a "straw man," an easy ideological target for cheap point-scoring. As wide and inclusive a range of viewpoints as possible is offered, with no privileging of one particular political ideology or cultural perspective over another. It is left to each individual reader to evaluate the relative merits of each argument—as he or she sees it, and with the use of ever-growing critical-thinking skills—and grapple with his or her own assumptions, beliefs, and perspectives to determine how convincing or successful any given argument is and how the reader's own stance on the issue may be modified or altered in response to it.

This process is facilitated and supported by volume, chapter, and selection introductions that provide readers with the essential context they need to begin engaging with the spotlighted issues, with the debates surrounding them, and with their own perhaps shifting or nascent opinions on them. In addition, guided reading and discussion questions encourage readers to determine the authors' point of view and purpose, interrogate and analyze the various arguments and their rhetoric and structure, evaluate the arguments' strengths and weaknesses, test their claims against available facts and evidence, judge the validity of the reasoning, and bring into clearer, sharper focus the reader's own beliefs and conclusions and how they may differ from or align with those in the collection or those of their classmates.

Research has shown that reading comprehension skills improve dramatically when students are provided with compelling, intriguing, and relevant "discussable" texts. The subject matter of these collections could not be more compelling, intriguing, or urgently relevant to today's students and the world they are poised to inherit. The anthologized articles and the reading and discussion questions that are included with them also provide the basis for stimulating, lively, and passionate classroom debates. Students who are compelled to anticipate objections to their own argument and identify the flaws in those of an opponent read more carefully, think more critically, and steep themselves in relevant context, facts, and information more thoroughly. In short, using discussable text of the kind provided by every single volume in the Opposing Viewpoints series encourages close reading, facilitates reading comprehension, fosters research, strengthens critical thinking, and greatly enlivens and energizes classroom discussion and participation. The entire learning process is deepened, extended, and strengthened.

For all of these reasons, Opposing Viewpoints continues to be exactly the right resource at exactly the right time—when we most need to provide readers with the critical-thinking tools and skills that will not only serve them well in school but also in their careers and their daily lives as decision-making family members, community members, and citizens. This series encourages respectful engagement with and analysis of opposing viewpoints and fosters a resulting increase in the strength and rigor of one's own opinions and stances. As such, it helps make readers "future ready," and that readiness will pay rich dividends for the readers themselves, for the citizenry, for our society, and for the world at large.

Introduction

> *"In 2018 alone, domestic extremists killed at least 50 people in the US, the fourth deadliest year on record for domestic extremist-related killings since 1970. Over the last ten years (2009-2018), right-wing extremists have been responsible for 73.3 percent of the 427 extremist-related murders in the US. By contrast, Islamic extremists were responsible for 23.4 percent."*
>
> —Anti-Defamation League

Ever since the notorious 9/11 attacks on the United States by Islamic terrorist group al-Qaeda in 2001, the focus of the US war on terror was Islamic terrorism. However, in recent years, another type of terrorism has come to the forefront. So-called "home-grown" domestic terrorism has emerged and even overshadowed the threat posed by radical Islam. Some of this terrorism has been a response to Islamic extremism; some has been directed at other minority groups, such as African Americans, gays, and Jews. And some has been issue-oriented, such as anti-abortion or environmental terrorism.

Domestic terrorism has created enough of a stir in the United States that the USA PATRIOT Act has expanded the definition of terrorism to cover "'domestic,' as opposed to international, terrorism." According to this revision, "A person engages in domestic terrorism if they do an act 'dangerous to human life' that is a violation of the criminal laws of a state or the United

States, if the act appears to be intended to: (i) intimidate or coerce a civilian population; (ii) influence the policy of a government by intimidation or coercion; or (iii) to affect the conduct of a government by mass destruction, assassination or kidnapping. Additionally, the acts have to occur primarily within the territorial jurisdiction of the United States...."[1]

Domestic terrorism has not been confined to the United States, however. Some of the more high-profile domestic mass murders of the twenty-first century have occurred on foreign soil. Among the most notorious were the 2011 attacks by Anders Behring Breivik. In a politically motivated attack, Breivik murdered 77 people at a summer camp in Norway. Hours before his attack, Breivik emailed a manifesto in which he raged against multiculturalism and the "threat" of Muslim immigration to Norway, as well as Marxism and the Norwegian Labor Party. He claimed to be a "savior of Christianity."[2]

A more recent high-profile attack occurred in Christchurch, New Zealand, on March 15, 2019. Brenton Tarrant, a 28-year-old white supremacist Australian, opened fire in two mosques, killing 51 people. Tarrant's attack was influenced by that of Breivik, and, like Breivik, he published a manifesto raving about the "replacement" of whites by non-white peoples.

Numerous recent examples of domestic terrorism have plagued the United States as well, but it would be a mistake to think that terrorism on US soil is a recent event. And neither political extreme, right or left, has a monopoly on domestic terrorism. In the past, such terrorism was often linked to far-left, anti-capitalist actors. Such was the case in 1910, when the *Los Angeles Times* building was bombed by a union member of the International Association of Bridge and Structural Iron Workers, who did so to protest capitalist oppression. In September 1920, a blast in the financial district of New York City killed thirty people and wounded over one hundred others. Now commonly referred to as the Wall Street bombing, the perpetrators were never found, though it has been speculated that it was the work of a group of anarchists. Left-wing violence once again reared its ugly head in the 1970s, when radical leftist groups such as the Weather Underground, the Black Panthers, the Black Liberation Army, the Symbionese Liberation Army, the New World Liberation Front, the FALN, the "Family," and the United Freedom Front were active. "According to FBI statistics, the United States experienced more than 2,500 domestic bombings in just 18 months in 1971 and 1972, with virtually no solved crimes and barely any significant prosecutions."[3]

Since that time, radical left-wing violence has dissipated and right-wing, white supremacist domestic terrorism has come to the forefront. Like left-wing terrorism, it has a long history. The twenty-first century has no monopoly on domestic terrorism. Among the most infamous right-wing domestic terrorist attacks was the Oklahoma City bombing by Timothy McVeigh and Terry Nichols in April 1995 that left 168 people dead. Another high-profile series of attacks was perpetrated by anti-abortion extremist Eric Rudolph, whose "work" includes the Atlanta Olympic bombing of 1996.

Even so, the aftermath of 9/11, and the rise of right-wing, nationalist, authoritarian ideologies worldwide has brought with it a spate of domestic terrorist incidents that have shocked both the United States and the world. A 2017 report to Congress by the United States Government Accountability Office determined that "Of the 85 violent extremist incidents that resulted in death since September 12, 2001, far right-wing violent extremist groups were responsible for 62,"[4] or 73 percent. It is no surprise that this violence coincides with the rise of the internet. The world wide web has provided a platform for extremists of all stripes to share their hatred, spew their bile, and find like-minded individuals, a very few of whom are not content to limit their activities to posting in online chat forums. Such individuals, radicalized online, act out their aggressions on the public, and lately, on innocent minority groups. In his deluded manifesto, Charleston church shooter Dylann Roof put it this way: "Well someone has to have the bravery to take it to the real world, and I guess that has to be me."[5]

Recent high profile domestic terrorist attacks have spurred fierce debate, giving rise to discussions about gun control, mental health, and even violence in the media. Included among these recent attacks are the Boston Marathon bombing of 2013, where two Kyrgyz-American brothers, Dzhokhar and Tamerlan Tsarnaev, were motivated by radical Islamist beliefs; the Charleston Church shooting, in which self-described white supremacist Dylann Roof murdered nine African-American churchgoers who had welcomed him into their Bible study group; the San Bernardino shooting of 2015, where an American citizen, Syed Rizwan Farook, and his wife, Tashfeen Malik, having been radicalized through jihadist internet sites, killed 14 people and wounded two dozen more; and the Orlando nightclub shooting of 2016, during which Omar Mateen murdered 59 at a gay nightclub in Orlando, Florida. Other even more recent attacks include the congressional baseball shooting of 2017, perpetrated by an alleged Bernie Sanders supporter; the 2017 Charlottesville car attack, during which a white supremacist killed one woman and injured 28 others; the Pittsburgh synagogue shooting of 2018; and the El Paso Walmart shooting, where Hispanics were targeted.

These events clearly run the political gamut: there are left-wing attacks, right-wing attacks, Islamic radical attacks. As suggested, no one group has a monopoly on domestic terrorism.

It is important also to note what is not domestic terrorism. Some of the more heinous crimes of the twenty-first century are not classified as domestic terrorism. These cases include the Sandy Hook Elementary School shooting, where Adam Lanza killed 20 six- and seven-year-olds and 6 adults; the Aurora, Colorado, massacre, in which James Eagon Holmes killed twelve people and wounded many more in a movie theater; and the 2017 Las Vegas shootings, where Stephen Paddock murdered 58 concertgoers. In all three cases, while the crime was certainly horrific, no political or social motive can be ascribed to the perpetrators. There was no attempt by these mass murderers to intimidate or coerce the public. None of the killers intended to influence or affect the conduct of the governments. Without such motivations, the crimes are not given domestic terror status.

While local and federal authorities have ramped up their efforts to combat mass killing events and domestic terrorists, there is no fail-safe method by which to ensure that domestic terrorists will not attack again and again. Such terrorists often choose so-called "soft targets," that attract great numbers of potential victims, such as concerts, holiday bazaars, and nightclubs.

It is clear that much work needs to be done to combat domestic terrorism in all of its guises. It remains to be seen how the current US administration will deal with—or fail to deal with—the imminent and ongoing threat of terror within its borders. In chapters titled "Is Domestic Terrorism a Major Concern?"; "Is Domestic Terrorism Ever Justified?"; "Are Politicians and the Media Stoking Domestic Terrorism?"; and "How Can Domestic Terrorism Be Prevented?,"*Opposing Viewpoints: Domestic Terrorism* presents a wide range of viewpoints concerning causes of domestic terrorism, whether it is being stoked by the media and politicians, and how best to confront it.

Endnotes

1. ACLU, "How the USA PATRIOT Act redefines 'Domestic Terrorism.'" https://www.aclu.org/other/how-usa-patriot-act-redefines-domestic-terrorism

2. Anders Behring Breivikhttps." Biography. April 2, 2014. https://www.biography.com/crime-figure/anders-behring-breivik

3. Eric Alterman, "Remembering the Left-Wing Terrorism of the 1970s." The Nation. April 14, 2015. https://www.thenation.com/article/remembering-left-wing-terrorism-1970s/

4. "Countering Violent Extremism: Actions Needed to Define Strategy and Assess Progress of Federal Efforts." US Government Accountability Office (GAO). Government Accountability Office, 6 Apr. 2017. https://www.gao.gov/assets/690/683984.pdf

5. Frances Robles. "Dylann Roof Photos and a Manifesto Are Posted on Website." *The New York Times*. June 20, 2015. https://www.nytimes.com/2015/06/21/us/dylann-storm-roof-photos-website-charleston-church-shooting.html

OPPOSING
VIEWPOINTS®
SERIES

CHAPTER 1

Is Domestic Terrorism a Major Concern?

Chapter Preface

There is no doubt that terrorism in general has been a major area of concern since the attacks on America of September 11, 2001. It was not the first attack on the United States by Islamic extremists (the World Trade Center had previously been bombed to lesser effect), nor would it be the last. Though such attacks have declined in recent years, America has probably not seen the last of this type of terrorism. But domestic terrorism, perpetrated by American citizens or those living in America on US soil, has seen a marked uptick. Has it assumed the proportions of a major security concern? The answer depends on whom one asks.

Those politically to the right of center would point to groups such as Antifa, to environmental terrorism, and to animal rights terrorism as legitimate concerns in twenty-first century America. Those to the left can reference the vastly more destructive attacks by white supremacists, anti-abortionists, anti-government groups, and other extreme right-wing elements that have plagued the country in the recent past. It would seem that the United States is under attack from within.

The US government recently made it official, according to Ellen Nakashima, national security reporter for *The Washington Post*. She writes that, "Domestic terrorism and mass attacks are as great a threat to the United States today as foreign terrorism, the Department of Homeland Security said in a new strategy report unveiled Friday."[1]

Some might say that the DHS is a little late to the party in waiting until September of 2019 to make such an obvious statement. Others might say that domestic terrorism has overtaken foreign terrorism as a threat.

One might wonder if what has held up a governmental response to domestic terrorism is the current administration itself. Many of the recent attacks, especially the high profile attacks, have been perpetrated by white nationalists. The Trump administration has said publically that it will do what necessary to counter white nationalist domestic terrorism. But privately, quietly, it has directed resources away from preventing such attacks. Writing for the *Los Angeles Times*, Molly O'Toole states that "the Department of Homeland Security, which is charged with identifying threats and preventing domestic terrorism, has sought to redirect resources away from countering anti-government, far-right and white supremacist groups."[2]

Instead, "Under Trump, 85% of the 'countering violent extremism' grants awarded by Homeland Security explicitly targeted Muslims and other minority groups, including immigrants and refugees."[3] One may well wonder how the United States will be able to counteract future attacks such as the El Paso Walmart massacre and the Pittsburgh Tree of Life synagogue shootings when the administration itself, by its own actions, has shown that it does not consider white supremacist domestic terrorism to be the scourge others have claimed it is. Will it take an internal attack on the order of 9/11 to spur the government to direct resources toward defeating domestic terrorism? One certainly hopes not.

Endnotes
1. Elleed-resources-from-countering-far-right-racism-fueled-domestic-terrorism

> *"...the legal definition of domestic terrorism includes any criminal act dangerous to human life that is 'intended to intimidate or coerce a civilian population' or 'to influence the policy of a government by intimidation or coercion.'"*

Defining Domestic Terrorism Is a Challenge

Josh Israel

In the following viewpoint Josh Israel writes that while the legal definition of domestic terrorism is absolutely clear, authorities have a hard time classifying acts that may constitute terrorism when politics are at play. If acts are committed by a non-Muslim, for example, authorities and certain politicians will not classify them as terrorist. Anti-abortion violence is one example of crimes that many on the right will label "mental health" issues but not terrorism. The author cites officials who believe that it is advantageous to label all such violent acts as domestic terrorism. Doing so allows those with expertise in mass attacks to address the problem. Additionally, resources can be employed beyond those typically associated with mental health issues. Josh Israel is a senior investigative reporter for ThinkProgress. Previously, he was a reporter and oversaw money-in-politics reporting at the Center for Public Integrity.

"Why Can't Anyone Agree on The Definition of 'Domestic Terrorism'?" by Josh Israel, Thinkprogress.org, December 9, 2015. Reprinted by permission.

As you read, consider the following questions:

1. Why was the task force that sought to define domestic terrorism dismantled?
2. How are Muslim terrorist acts and right-wing extremist attacks handled differently?
3. Why is it more practical to see anti-abortion offenders as part of a larger group than as lone wolves?

After last month's attack on a Planned Parenthood clinic in Colorado Springs, Colorado left three people dead and nine more wounded, information about the suspect's anti-abortion ideology quickly emerged. According to recent reports, the man arrested in the killings, Robert Dear, asked for directions to the clinic on the day of the shooting and told investigators, "No more baby parts" in the aftermath of the attack.

Despite evidence to the contrary, House Homeland Security Committee Chairman Michael McCaul (R-TX) said on ABC's *This Week* that he did not believe the shootings constituted terrorism. "It's, I think, a mental health crisis. I don't think it would fall under quite the definition of domestic terrorism," he said, though he noted he would "leave that to the Justice Department to make that determination."

Others, including Planned Parenthood, Colorado Gov. John Hickenlooper (D), Colorado Springs Mayor John Suthers (R), and even former Gov. Mike Huckabee (R-AR) took the opposite view, calling it "domestic terrorism" and "absolutely abominable."

The attack came just two days after NARAL Pro-Choice America and more than 100 other organizations and providers wrote to the US Department of Justice to ask that anti-abortion violence be officially treated as domestic terrorism. They noted that the legal definition of domestic terrorism includes any criminal act dangerous to human life that is "intended to intimidate or coerce a civilian population" or "to influence the policy of a government by intimidation or coercion"—a definition that seems to very clearly include the Colorado Springs shooting.

Less than a week later, the death toll in Colorado Springs was eclipsed by yet another mass shooting—this time by an American-born man who reportedly claims to be Muslim and his Pakistani-born wife. Within days, the FBI announced that this case was being handled as a terrorism case. On Sunday, President Obama delivered a national address from the Oval Office outlining "steps that we can take together to defeat the terrorist threat," focusing almost exclusively on ISIS-related terrorism.

But should a radical anti-abortion extremist's attacks also be officially classified as acts of domestic terrorism? And why does it matter? ThinkProgress reached out to abortion rights advocates, national security experts, and academics who study anti-abortion violence and asked them these questions. Their answers revealed an opaque governmental process for handling a growing trend of threats, arsons, bombings, and shootings targeting women's health clinics and doctors.

Administrative Caution

In 2009, the US Department of Homeland Security (DHS) produced an assessment titled, "Rightwing Extremism: Current Economic and Political Climate Fueling Resurgence in Radicalization and Recruitment," which warned that the combination of the nation's economic downturn and the recent inauguration of the first African American president of the United States could "present unique drivers for rightwing radicalization and recruitment." It specifically noted that this extremism could include "groups and individuals that are dedicated to a single issue, such as opposition to abortion or immigration."

Conservatives were not pleased. Jay Sekulow of the American Center for Law and Justice denounced the inclusion of anti-abortion extremists, asking, "Why would the Department of Homeland Security single out groups like pro-life supporters when they should be focusing on identifying and apprehending the real terrorists—

like al-Qaeda—groups that have vowed to destroy America?" The Liberty Counsel defiantly distributed "Right-Wing Extremist" cards to its supporters. Then-House Republican Leader John Boehner (R-OH) demanded to know why DHS Secretary Janet Napolitano "has abandoned using the term 'terrorist' to describe those, such as al Qaeda, who are plotting overseas to kill innocent Americans, while her own Department is using the same term to describe American citizens who disagree with the direction Washington Democrats are taking our nation."

The report was soon withdrawn and the team that created it was reportedly "effectively eviscerated."

Daryl Johnson, who was lead analyst for domestic terrorism at the Department of Homeland Security from 2004 to 2010 and the primary author of the report, told ThinkProgress that the federal government, for the past several years, has been hesitant to label acts of domestic terrorism as such. "There seems to be a disconnect as to what constitutes terrorism within government, particularly if it's of the non-Muslim variety," he said. And while there is a lot of attention given by the public and the media to the ISIS threat, "to date we have had very few incidents of ISIS-related terrorism in the United States, compared to all of the incidents related to terrorist plotting we've had this year."

Heidi Beirich, director of the Southern Poverty Law Center's Intelligence Project, echoed this view. "Until recently, under the Obama administration there had been a real reluctance to brand almost anything that looks like domestic terrorism as domestic terrorism," she said. But Beirich pointed to two recent developments that could signal a shift within the federal government: In June 2014, then-Attorney General Eric Holder revived a long-dormant domestic terrorism task force (created after the 1995 Oklahoma City bombing but lapsed after September 11, 2001) and in October, Assistant Attorney General John Carlin announced a newly created Domestic Terrorism Counsel position to coordinate domestic terrorism cases and prevention.

WHAT IS THE THREAT TO THE US TODAY?

The main terrorist threat today in the United States is best understood as emerging from across the political spectrum, as ubiquitous firearms, political polarization, and other factors have combined with the power of online communication and social media to generate a complex and varied terrorist threat that crosses ideologies and is largely disconnected from traditional understandings of terrorist organizations.

No jihadist foreign terrorist organization has directed a deadly attack inside the United States since 9/11, and no deadly jihadist attacker has received training or support from groups abroad. In the almost 18 years after 9/11, jihadists have killed 104 people inside the United States. This death toll is virtually the same as that from far-right terrorism (consisting of anti-government, white supremacist, and anti-abortion violence), which has killed 109 people. The United States has also seen attacks in recent years inspired by ideological misogyny and black separatist/nationalist ideology. Individuals motivated by these ideologies have killed eight people each. America's terrorism problem today is homegrown and is not the province of any one group or ideological perspective.

Lack of Transparency

In 2011, a Huffington Post report raised concerns that the National Counterterrorism Center had released a database of terrorist attacks globally, between 2004 and 2010, that appeared to omit most anti-abortion-related attacks over that time.

But the official determination of whether an incident is "domestic terrorism" is made by the FBI, Johnson explained, and that information is not always released to the public. "The 'Terrorism in the United States' report that used to come out annually has not existed since 2005," so there's no official US government document or report annually to let the public know what the FBI deems as terrorism," he said. "That's what's led to a lot of the confusion today."

While the United States has seen a series of deadly attacks by individuals and pairs inspired by jihadism, the United States today is a hard target for foreign terrorist organizations, which have not directed and carried out a successful deadly attack in the country since 9/11. This is the result of a layered set of defenses including tips from local communities, members of the public, and the widespread use of informants.

A deadly attack directed from abroad cannot be ruled out. For example, the 2009 Christmas Day bomb plot by Umar Farouk Abdulmuttalab—who was trained and directed by Al Qaeda in the Arabian Peninsula—failed only because the explosive didn't work. The Times Square bomb plot by Faisal Shahzad, who in 2010 managed to place a car bomb in Times Square undetected after training with the Pakistani Taliban, which again did not detonate properly, is another example. Despite these cases, the most likely threat continues to be lone individuals or pairs inspired by jihadist ideology without the type of extensive plotting, communication, or travel activity that would tip off the layered counterterrorism defense system.

"Part IV. What is the Threat to the United States Today?" New America.

"By calling it terrorism, you are not only alerting the public to an issue, but for statistical purposes, it gives us a data point to analyze the current and future threat," Johnson observed. In 2012 testimony to the Senate Judiciary Committee's constitution subcommittee, Johnson urged that his annual report be revived.

The Department of Justice did not respond to numerous ThinkProgress inquiries about its determination process.

Sasha Bruce, senior vice president of campaigns and strategy for NARAL, told ThinkProgress that the campaign to urge DOJ to officially classify attacks on abortion providers as acts of domestic terrorism is rooted in a desire for transparency. "Our push is not with the assumption that they are doing the wrong thing," she said. "It's that we don't know that they're doing the right thing. So many investigations happen behind closed doors, we're asking that they give public assurance that they're doing the right thing… we're just asking for an indication that they are considering domestic terrorism [as they investigate attacks like Colorado Springs]."

Kathy Spillar, executive director of the Feminist Majority Foundation, said that while the FBI may not be classifying these incidents as domestic terrorism, the number of attacks has been disturbingly high and increasing.

"We're living in a time where more than half of providers are experiencing real threats: doctors being featured on WANTED posters, clinic staffs being stalked in their homes, callers threatening to blow the clinic up or kill a person," Spillar explained. "These threats often end in acts of violence."

Her organization's National Clinic Access Project tracks threats against clinics that provide abortion. It found that almost one in five clinics experienced severe violence last year—a largely unchanged statistic since the late 1990s. Recently, the number of clinics impacted by threats and intimidation has climbed from 26.6 percent in 2010 to 51.9 percent in 2014.

Why It Matters: The Practical and the Political

While Spillar says we need "aggressive enforcement and clear statements by public officials that abortion is legal and should not be the target of extremists who commit violence and go on suicide missions to do it," she is not certain that doing that necessarily requires classifying those acts as terrorism.

But David S. Cohen, a professor of law at Drexel University, told ThinkProgress that while the Department of Justice under President Obama has been working diligently to prosecute clinic violence, the terrorism designation could still help them do the job even better. If a clinic attack is officially classified as domestic terrorism, he noted, "it can be treated different by the federal government and more resources might be available." In addition to the Department of Justice's Civil Rights Division, which handles abortion clinic attacks, the designation would mean that the domestic terrorism unit would also become involved. And that could bring "an additional way of thinking about it, tracking, and understanding of information," he added.

NARAL's Bruce agreed, noting that the divisions have different resources and expertise. "The people who work in domestic terrorism have different expertise than those who work on Freedom of Access to Clinic Entrances Act charges every day," she said. "Are they applicable? Perhaps. Given how prevalent [these attacks] are and the fact that they are increasing, we'd look to them for as many [types of expertise] as possible."

Alesha E. Doan, who chairs the Women, Gender, and Sexuality Studies Department at the University of Kansas, pointed to another reason why calling it domestic terrorism matters: framing.

"The importance to framing [anti-abortion attacks] as political violence, acts of violence that exist in the political conversation, has material outcomes in terms of policy," she said. "Traditionally, in the last four decades, these acts of violence have largely been framed [by abortion opponents as] a mentally disturbed individual, a lone wolf," she added, though these violent extremists exist within the anti-abortion movement.

According to Doan, seeing the attacks as part of that broader context "would place a focus on the language, the inflammatory rhetoric that our politicians and political actors use." That gives the anti-abortion activists and their political supporters "a very large political stake in discounting this violence as just random violence. And really, there's nothing random about it."

Bruce noted that, regardless of whether it's called terrorism, it is important that an attack like the one that took place in Colorado Springs is not dismissed as a lone-wolf attack unrelated to the "hate-filled rhetoric" that preceded it.

"[Abortion-rights opponents are] going out of their way to say the pro-choice movement is trying to tie this to the anti-abortion movement coming out of the right," she said, "which we are, because we think this it is connected and they are going out of their way to say that it's not."

"We're not saying everybody is a murderer. But they are connected, you don't get to align yourself with [those who say] it's justifiable to kill abortion doctors—and then say acts like this aren't connected to you."

> *"I'm a gun-rights supporter and own some legally purchased and properly stored firearms, and they are no threat to anything—other than the errant coyote who attacks my herd of goats, or any potential home invader."*

White Nationalists Pose a Serious Threat

Steven Greenhut

In the following viewpoint, Steven Greenhut defends his right to own arms, but then veers into a discussion of recent mass shootings. While not all attacks have been perpetrated by white nationalists, he states, it is clear that America has a problem with this type of violence. Greenhut suggests steps to deal with the problem. As for passing new laws to deal with right-wing terrorists, Greenhut does not agree. He believes that it will be far more effective to use existing laws to combat the problem. Steven Greenhut is the California columnist for the San Diego Union-Tribune. *He formerly was vice president of journalism at the Franklin Center for Government and Public Integrity. He is the author of* Abuse of Power: How the Government Misuses Eminent Domain *and* Plunder! How Public Employee Unions are Raiding Treasuries, Controlling Our Lives and Bankrupting the Nation.

"Yes, America Faces a Threat from White Nationalists. No, More Laws Won't Fix That." by Steven Greenhut, Reason Foundation, August 16, 2019. Reprinted by permission.

As you read, consider the following questions:

1. What clichés does the author use to support his argument?
2. How does the rhetoric of politicians need to change to reduce mass violence, according to the viewpoint?
3. What are some solutions to right-wing violence offered by the author?

As the cliché goes, "guns don't kill people, people kill people." I'm a gun-rights supporter and own some legally purchased and properly stored firearms, and they are no threat to anything— other than the errant coyote who attacks my herd of goats, or any potential home invader. Still, we all need to face the fact that people armed with powerful weapons can cause a hell of a lot of carnage.

That's why the latest mass shootings are so upsetting. Your family is at a wholesome community festival, or doing some back-to-school shopping and, in the blink of an eye, you're in a scene from war-torn Beirut. This is not a column about gun control. I will evaluate specific proposals as they are unveiled, but this column is about why some people—using high-capacity rifles or whatnot—commit atrocities.

If your neighbor were unbalanced, armed to the teeth and busy posting social-media messages about how much he hates you, you'd certainly support measures to disarm him. But you'd feel more secure if he didn't hate you in the first place. Here's another cliché: "Ideas matter." The people using guns to slaughter people are, in most cases, driven by ideas. What are those ideas and why do they matter? Why do they hate you?

"If foreign terrorists attacked Dayton, El Paso and Gilroy, would America do nothing?" asked a USA Today editorial's headline. Indeed. When it comes to Islamic radical terror, Americans aren't fuzzy headed. They don't ruminate about the need for mental-health services or question the reason why some of these killers stage horrific attacks.

I recall a comedy routine in which the actors, pretending to be TV anchors, try to figure out the reasons for an act of terrorism. They read the Arabic names of the attackers and pretended to be stumped by the motivation for the violence. It was an apparent jab at former President Obama for his reluctance to use the term "Islamic terrorism."

Now, we've got a similar situation on the right. Not all, but some of the latest mass killers appear motivated by a far-right, white-nationalist ideology. A manifesto posted online shortly before the El Paso shooting spree, which may have been penned by the alleged shooter, railed against "the Hispanic invasion of Texas" and worried about "cultural and ethnic replacement."

The suspect in the shooting death of 11 worshipers at a Pittsburgh, Pennsylvania, synagogue last year allegedly told the police, "They're committing genocide to my people. I just want to kill Jews." We're familiar with the fatal car attack at the white nationalist rally in Charlottesville, Virginia, and the 2015 attack on an African-American church in Charleston, South Carolina, that left nine people dead.

Obviously, not all of the recent mass shootings are the work of right-wing fanatics. Last weekend's alleged shooter in Dayton, Ohio, reportedly had made left-wing posts on social media. One of the most infamous, politically motivated murder sprees was the work of the Unabomber, who penned a 35,000-word screed against modern industrial society. I remember conservatives noting the similarity of his ideas to those of Al Gore.

Despite Fox News anchor Tucker Carlson's claim that the nation's white-supremacy problem is a hoax, the evidence suggests otherwise. It's not the nation's only violence problem. But conservatives, including Donald Trump, were quick to pinpoint the reason for, say, a mass shooting in San Bernardino, California, that killed 14 people at a Christmas party. The then-presidential candidate called for a "total and complete shutdown of Muslims entering the United States until our country's representatives can figure out what the hell is going on."

Why is it so difficult to call out what's going on now? I'm not blaming the president for recent violence, although I wish he would knock off the incendiary rhetoric about immigrants. Everyone should tone down the hysterics and anger, which only motivates the nutcases among us.

But the president and some of his supporters have a blind spot about white-nationalist terror, just as the former president had a blind spot about Islamic radicalism. The president's recent talk was more presidential than usual, as he condemned "racism, bigotry and white supremacy," but then he undermined his points with subsequent Twitter tirades.

There's clearly an energized group of self-radicalized white nationalists who "take inspiration from prior acts of vicious mayhem and cheer high body counts on Internet message boards," wrote National Review's Rich Lowry. He called on the FBI to treat these "domestic terrorists and subversives" in the way that they crushed what was once America's most notorious hate group, the Ku Klux Klan.

Using existing laws to stamp out potentially violent extremists is a better starting point than passing new laws that mostly target law-abiding citizens. That means acknowledging that people who kill people with guns often are motivated by twisted ideologies. It's time to confront those ideologies, whether they emanate from the white-nationalist right, Islamic radical movements or any other fever swamp.

> "*Ultimately, as it's been observed many times, the violence you reap abroad is the violence you eventually sow at home.*"

The Domestic Terrorism Problem Is Eclipsing Foreign Terrorism

C. J. Werleman

In the following viewpoint C. J. Werleman writes that in recent times, domestic violence has begun to eclipse the threat posed by foreign attackers. This wave can be attributed to a period of religious extremist violence currently in effect. Werleman states that the predominant conspiracy theory at the core of right-wing extremism contends that there is a Jewish plot to overrun Western countries with immigrants. According to Werleman, President Trump helps perpetuate this absurd conspiracy theory. The United States. has waged war in eighty countries abroad; according to Werleman, it has now unleashed such a war at home. C. J. Werleman is a journalist, author, and analyst on conflict and terrorism. He is the author of Crucifying America, God Hates You. Hate Him Back, *and* Koran Curious.

"Is White Extremism the Biggest Domestic Terror Threat in the US?" by CJ Werleman, TRT World, July 2, 2019. Reprinted by permission.

As you read, consider the following questions:

1. According to David C. Rapoport, what are "Four Waves of Modern Terrorism"?
2. What effect has the internet had on modern terrorism?
3. What role does anti-Semitism play in domestic terrorism?

For years US terror warnings have focused on groups like Al Qaeda or Daesh, but the latest warnings from US law enforcement agencies point to homegrown terrorists as the most immediate danger.

The United States has been in a permanent state of war since the attacks of September 11, 2001, finding itself voluntarily involved in military operations and theatres that span multiple continents. A war-weary American public has become accustomed to the routine terror warnings issued by law enforcement agencies in advance of national holidays and major sporting events.

The coming 4th of July festivities to celebrate the country's independence from Britain, however, marks a new reality in its never-ending and self-defeating "War on Terror."

Previous terror warnings issued by federal authorities over nearly two decades have focused on the threat posed by groups and individuals inspired or associated with overseas groups, such as ISIS (Daesh) and Al Qaeda.

This year, a joint intelligence bulletin issued by the FBI, Department of Homeland Security and National Counterterrorism Center warns that domestic terrorists who have been radicalised by white supremacy and opposition to abortion could look to attack Independence Day revellers.

Essentially, the US now finds itself standing face-to-face with a white domestic terrorism crisis, a psychosis that can only be brought upon by a permanent state of war.

Professor David C. Rapoport, an internationally acclaimed terrorism scholar, described what has become known as the "Four Waves of Modern Terrorism." These waves are marked by his identification of the primary global terror threat from the end of the 19th century until today, with anarchists identified as such at the beginning of the 20th century; anti-colonialists during the post-Second World War period; the New Left during the 1970s; and religious extremists from 1979 until now.

Essentially, what Rapoport is describing is how terrorism threats exist within their own life cycle, spurred on by global socio-economic-political realities, and with cataclysmic political events in the Middle East and the negative consequences of globalisation blamed for the rise of global violent "jihadist" movements.

The threat of religious extremism is forecasted to dissipate by 2025, based on the assumption that the generational life cycle for each wave remains constant, but it appears self-evident the fifth wave is already upon us—that being the threat of white domestic terrorists.

From Pittsburgh to San Diego; from Charleston to Quebec City; from London to Christchurch, violent right-wing extremists are shooting up mosques, synagogues, and black churches at the same time hate crimes against Muslims, Jews, and immigrants are spiking upwards.

If this reality needs further emphasis, then consider that right-wing extremists are responsible for 100 percent of all acts of terrorism in the US since the end of 2017, a statistic that doesn't include the ever-increasing number of foiled far-right terror plots.

The terror warning issued for July 4 celebrations by Federal authorities mentioned the case of James Field, the white supremacist who ploughed his car into a crowd of counter-protesters in Charlottesville, Virginia, which left one woman dead and dozens injured.

Last month, the FBI announced that it's currently tracking 850 possible domestic terrorists within the US, adding that the number of cases targeting white nationalists and other racially motivated extremists has jumped in the past six months.

"In fact, there have been more arrests and deaths in the United States caused by domestic terrorists than international terrorists in recent years," Assistant Director Michael McGarrity, the head of the FBI's counterterrorism division, told a Congressional House panel in May.

He added that "mobilisation to violence is much quicker" today because the hatred and extremist ideologies are spreading more widely and rapidly online.

More alarming is the fact that the Christchurch mosque terrorist attack, which left 51 Muslim worshippers dead, has become the "blue ribbon" event for right-wing extremists in the same way 9/11 became Muslim extremists, insofar as the ability of both to inspire copy cat attacks and draw recruits.

"Attacks always spark reactions from different extremist communities, but when it comes to the far right, there was never anything like the response to the Christchurch attack," Rita Katz, director of SITE Intelligence Group, told The Sun-Herald, adding that the gunman's targeting of Muslims, coupled with his "deadly execution" and live streaming of the attack has generated an "unprecedented response."

"It's like nothing we've ever seen thus far from the far-right across the globe," he said.

The predominant conspiracy theory at the core of right-wing extremism is one that contends there's a Jewish plot to overrun Western countries with immigrants, particularly Muslims, so that liberal and multicultural "globalist" elites may rule over the democratic political world.

Dangerously, the current President of the United States perpetuates this racist conspiracy by routinely portraying the US to be under attack from Muslims and immigrants, while at the same time of boasting of being a "nationalist."

Trump's ban on Muslim immigrants and proposed wall along the US-Mexico border are served up as political rewards for far-right extremists, who constitute his political base.

When you consider how Robert Bowers, the right-wing extremist who killed eleven Jewish worshipers at a synagogue in Pittsburgh last year, blamed a Jewish refugee organisation ("Evil

Jews") for "bringing in the (sic) Filthy EVIL Muslims into the country," you can see how the political demonisation of religious minorities and immigrants manifests into violence in the streets.

Ultimately, as it's been observed many times, the violence you reap abroad is the violence you eventually sow at home.

For the nearly eighteen years now, the US has waged military operations in eighty countries, and in doing so has unleashed and fueled violent insurgencies in Iraq, Afghanistan, Yemen, Pakistan, Somalia and elsewhere.

It appears now the US has unleashed one at home.

> *"Far from beating back the white supremacist movement, antifa is pouring fuel on the racist fire."*

Antifa Is Not a Domestic Terrorist Group, But It Is Still a Problem

Scott Stewart

In the following viewpoint, Scott Stewart argues that despite violent acts associated with Antifa (short for Anti-Fascist Action), it cannot be labeled a terrorist organization because it is not really an organized group. Antifa, Stewart explains, is actually a campaign that encompasses a wide variety of movements with varying ideologies. Nevertheless, Antifa does promote the use of "direct action"—which may include harassment, intimidation and violence against its right-wing opponents. Given their penchant for violence, Stewart writes, certain members of Antifa, especially anarchistic types, can be as odious as those they oppose. Antifa poses a significant problem to members of society who get in its way, but it is not a terrorist group. Scott Stewart supervises analysis of terrorism and security issues for Stratfor, a company that specializes in geopolitical intelligence. He was formerly a special agent with the US State Department for ten years and was involved in hundreds of terrorism investigations.

"Examining Whether the Terrorism Label Applies to Antifa," by Scott Stewart, Stratfor Enterprises, LLC, August 27, 2019. https://worldview.stratfor.com/article/why-terrorist-label-doesnt-apply-antifa-portland-white-supremacism is republished with the permission of Stratfor, a leading global geopolitical intelligence and advisory firm.

As you read, consider the following questions:

1. How is Antifa different from traditional terrorist groups?
2. What is the history of anarchism in the United States?
3. Why are some Antifa members as odious as the fascists they oppose, according to the author?

In 2017, Oxford Dictionaries shortlisted it as one of its words of the year, and since then, the term has become arguably even more prominent. Indeed, antifa (Anti-Fascist Action) seems to be everywhere these days. An anarchist associated with antifa was shot and killed by police on July 13 as he carried a rifle and attempted to burn buses and a propane tank at an immigration detention center in Tacoma, Washington. On August 4, a man who associated with antifa killed nine people in a mass shooting outside a bar in Dayton, Ohio, having previously carried a similar rifle while participating in a local counterprotest against the Ku Klux Klan on March 25. And on August 17, a large group of antifa and other counterprotesters rallied to oppose a gathering of white supremacists in Portland in the latest in a long string of confrontations between antifa and white supremacists in the Oregon city. The event drew widespread media coverage—although it wasn't just the press that was watching. Prior to the event, US President Donald Trump tweeted that authorities were giving "major consideration" to naming antifa an "organization of terror." Portland police largely succeeded in keeping the two sides apart, but they did detain 13 people (mostly antifa-linked anarchists) after the white supremacists left the city.

Anti-Fascist Action, better known as antifa, has made a name for itself in opposing white supremacist and neo-Nazi organizations, yet that does not necessarily make much of what it does virtuous, particularly as elements within the movement frequently engage in activity that harms people or property. Understanding what antifa is, and is not, can help people understand the threat it poses.

But does all of that make antifa a terrorist organization? The short answer is no—if for no other reason that antifa isn't really a group or organization to begin with. That, however, doesn't mean that some who have adopted the ideological mantle of anti-fascism do not engage in terrorist or militant activity—something that could have profound implications for anyone caught in the middle of a battle between antifa and the far-right.

Amorphous Antifa

Far from being a single group or organization, antifa is more a campaign featuring a wide array of movements, "affinity groups" (anarchist shorthand for operational cells) and individuals subscribing to various ideologies who band together to oppose neo-Nazis, white supremacists and others they consider to be fascists. Antifa, accordingly, doesn't have a single unified and overarching ideology that binds participants together other than their joint opposition to fascism. That said, antifa as a movement does openly promote the use of "direct action"—which can take the form of harassment, intimidation and violence against its right-wing opponents. But while many of those who participate in antifa actions do hold ideologies that condone political violence, including terrorism, this is not a universal belief, meaning conflict between people of various ideologies inside antifa protests is not uncommon. In Portland, for instance, anarchists severely beat an antifa participant for criticizing their indiscriminate violence.

Anarchists, along with Marxists, Maoists and anarcho-syndicalists, are usually among the most visible, vocal and violent elements that participate in antifa protests. Their respective black, red, and red-and-black flags are a ubiquitous sight at antifa gatherings, and it is no coincidence that many participants wear clothing with the same colors. The anarchist Black Bloc contingent, for example, is usually conspicuous at protests due to its dress, flags and the violence it leaves in its wake.

Ultimately, there is a long history of anarchist terrorism, both in the United States and around the world. And it is not just a thing

TRUMP ON ANTIFA

US President Donald Trump said his administration is giving "major consideration" for listing the US-based Antifa, short for "anti-fascists", a domestic terror group.

"Major consideration is being given to naming ANTIFA an 'ORGANIZATION OF TERROR.'," Trump said in a tweet on Sunday and warned the officials at the city of Portland, the home of Rose City, the oldest and most active Antifa group in the US.

"Portland is being watched very closely," Trump said and advised the mayor of Portland to "properly" do his job.

Scott Crow, one of the former Antifa organizers, told CNN in 2017 that the idea of Antifa is to curb hate speech wherever it happens if it is endangering people's lives.

"The idea in Antifa is that we go where they [right-wing] go. That hate speech is not free speech," Crow said.

"And so we go to cause conflict, to shut them down where they are, because we don't believe that Nazis or fascists of any stripe should have a mouthpiece," Crow added, defending Antifa's no-platforming tactic.

Since the election of Donald Trump as president of the US, a number of Antifa protesters is on the rise, comprised of mainly young, progressive, liberal and left-wing Americans.

Conservative groups in the US slam Antifa groups for being violent during protests and hampering free speech.

Antifa idea is traced to Nazi Germany and Anti-Fascist Action, a militant group founded in the 1980s in the United Kingdom.

"US: Anti-Fascist Group Might Be Labelled 'Terror Group,'" by Vakkas Dogantekin, Anadolu Agency.

of the past. Anarchists frequently mail parcel bombs or conduct fire bombings or other attacks in Mexico, South America and Europe, and many also plan and stage terrorist attacks inside the United States. The Tacoma and Dayton incidents, accordingly, were not the first anarchist attacks to occur in America. Of course, history is also replete with examples of Marxist militancy in the

United States and elsewhere from groups such as the Weather Underground and the Fuerzas Armadas de Liberacion Nacional (both in the United States), the Revolutionary Armed Forces of Colombia, the Red Army Faction (Germany) and the Red Brigades (Italy), among many others.

A Battle Going Back to Nazi Times

The history of anarchist and communist opposition to fascism is nearly a century old, particularly in regard to Adolf Hitler's Germany and Benito Mussolini's Italy. In Germany, the specter of communism, as evidenced by the domestic public's reaction to the alleged communist involvement in the 1933 Reichstag fire, directly contributed to Hitler's rise to power. And beyond the mere implications for Spain, the 1936-1939 Spanish Civil War pitted the global anarchist and communist movements against Europe's fascist states. This leftist opposition to fascism continued through World War II, when communists and anarchists proved to be some of the most successful anti-Nazi partisan fighters in places like Italy, Greece, France and Yugoslavia. After the war, these leftists remained a potent force—even forming the government in Yugoslavia.

In the end, both fascists and communists/anarchists strived to dominate the world based on diametrically opposed utopian narratives: the Aryan Third Reich versus an international workers' paradise. Both of these ideologies opposed—and continue to do so—the current bourgeois political and capitalist economic system in the United States and the West. They seek to overthrow the current world systems with new orders, which is why it is no surprise that anarchists and communists—whatever their enduring differences of opinion on how to organize society—detest the police as representatives of the state and frequently clash with them during protests. During demonstrations, they also often vandalize businesses and destroy property belonging to multinational companies.

Far from beating back the white supremacist movement, antifa is pouring fuel on the racist fire.

Eliciting Sympathy for the Devil

Is it wrong to oppose neo-Nazis and other white supremacists? No. But that does not make the more violent aspects of the antifa movement a noble undertaking, as both parties in a conflict can be odious. By way of example, look no further than the battle between the Islamic State and al Qaeda, which disproves the old adage that the enemy of my enemy is my friend.

Furthermore, the methods that antifa participants use to oppose white supremacists are clearly at odds with the US Constitution, which grants everyone—no matter how reprehensible their speech is—the right to speak freely or assemble without facing the prospect of physical violence. What's more, antifa's actions against groups such as the Proud Boys and Patriot Prayer not only generate massive amounts of publicity for these extreme organizations, but also sympathy. This benefits white supremacists more than it hurts them—illustrating why they continue to conduct marches in places like Portland, where the well-organized local antifa scene will inevitably take the bait and assault them, reinforcing their narrative that they are an oppressed group. In this way, far from beating back the white supremacist movement, antifa is pouring fuel on the racist fire.

But even if elements that participate in the antifa movement espouse political violence to oppose white supremacists, that doesn't make it a terrorist group—presidential threats to declare it one notwithstanding. Nevertheless, the more forceful aspects of the ideology's direct action are likely to result in disorder on the streets and damage to property, presenting a problem for any person or business that happens to find itself in the way.

> "As one anti-abortion extremist, while serving a prison sentence for anti-abortion arsons, put it in 2010: 'Abortionists are killed because they are serial murderers of innocent children who must be stopped, and they will continue to be stopped.'"

Anti-Abortion Violence Is America's Forgotten Domestic Terrorism

The Anti-Defamation League

In the following viewpoint the Anti-Defamation League argues that while much attention has been paid to Muslim terrorist acts, anti-abortion violence has for the most part flown under the media's radar. The authors trace the history of recent anti-abortion violence and provide a list of major incidents in the twenty-first century. Anti-abortion violence is often excluded from official US government lists of terrorism, which gives the impression that it is not a significant problem. The Anti-Defamation League is an international Jewish non-governmental organization based in the United States. Its mission is to fight anti-Semitism and all forms of bigotry.

As you read, consider the following questions:

1. What is "single-issue" extremism?
2. When did anti-abortion violence peak, according to the viewpoint?
3. What are some recent examples of anti-abortion violence?

In recent years, domestic extremists of various stripes have committed violent acts in the United States from murders to arsons to bombings. The perpetrators garnering the most attention, from both the media and the government, have been domestic Muslim extremists. Right-wing anti-government extremists and white supremacists have come in second. Attention has also been devoted to the violent acts of environmental and animal rights extremists.

The recent arrest in Green Bay, Wisconsin, of Francis Grady, 50, for allegedly setting off an incendiary device at a Planned Parenthood clinic serves to remind Americans of another form of domestic extremism: anti-abortion violence. Like environmental and animal rights violence, anti-abortion violence is a form of single-issue extremism. Typically, single-issue extremism emerges as an ultra-radical wing of a much broader social or political movement, a wing so agitated about its chosen cause that its adherents may come to believe that violence in the service of that cause is justified or even required.

The radical anti-abortion movement emerged in the 1980s; its violence peaked in the early 1990s with dozens of bombings, arsons, murders and attempted murders. The frequency of anti-abortion violence began to ebb in the mid-1990s, but never dissipated entirely. Anti-abortion violence has actually remained a consistent, if secondary, source of domestic terrorism and violence, manifesting itself most often in assaults and vandalism, with occasional arsons, bombings, drive-by shootings, and assassination attempts. As one anti-abortion extremist, while serving a prison sentence for anti-abortion arsons, put it in 2010: "Abortionists are killed because they are serial murderers of innocent children who must be stopped, and they will continue to be stopped."

In addition to the Green Bay firebombing, some other recent examples of anti-abortion violence include:

- Madison, Wisconsin, March 2012: A federal grand jury indicted Ralph Lang, 63, on charges of attempting to intimidate by force people participating in a program receiving federal financial assistance, as well as using or carrying a firearm in relation to the alleged crime. According to police, Lang travelled to Madison to threaten to kill people at a local Planned Parenthood clinic; he was arrested after allegedly firing his gun in a motel room while practicing drawing it.
- Pensacola, Florida, February 2012: A federal grand jury indicted Bobby Joe Rogers, 41, of Pensacola, Florida, for the alleged arson of a women's health clinic in Pensacola the previous month. Rogers allegedly used a Molotov cocktail (a type of incendiary device) to set the fire.
- Madera, California, January 2012: A federal court sentenced Donny Eugene Mower, 38, to five years in prison for having thrown a Molotov cocktail at a Planned Parenthood clinic in Madera in 2010, leaving behind a note that read, in part, "Let's see if you can burn just as well as your victims."
- McKinney, Texas, July 2011: A Molotov cocktail was thrown at a Planned Parenthood clinic in north Texas.
- Greensboro, North Carolina, March 2011: Justin Carl Moose, 26, received a 30-month federal prison sentence after pleading guilty to distributing information pertaining to the manufacturing and use of an explosive. Moose, who claimed to be part of the radical anti-abortion group Army of God, had described himself as an "extremist radical fundamentalist" who wanted to fight abortion "by any means necessary and at any cost." He had provided bomb-making instructions to an undercover FBI informant whom he thought was going to bomb an abortion clinic.

- Wichita, Kansas, April 2010: A federal court sentenced anti-abortion extremist Scott Roeder to life in prison on first degree murder and aggravated assault charges for the June 2009 assassination of a Wichita physician who performed abortion procedures.
- Plano, Texas, April 2010: FBI agents arrested Erlydon Lo, 27, on charges that he threatened to use deadly force against a women's clinic in Dallas. Lo had filed a document threatening to appear at the facility the next day that said, in part, "if I must use deadly force to defend the innocent life of another human being, I will."
- St. Paul, Minnesota, May 2009: Matthew Lee Derosia, 33, received a sentence of time serviced and five years of probation for purposely driving his truck earlier that year into the front of a St. Paul Planned Parenthood clinic on the anniversary of the Supreme Court decision of *Roe v. Wade*.

Unfortunately, incidents of anti-abortion violence are often excluded from government reports on terrorism in the United States, which can easily help create an impression that it is no longer a problem. On the contrary, anti-abortion violence remains a troubling element of America's domestic terrorism environment.

> "The pro-abortionists know full well that we are right—they are killing babies, their consciences are stinging over it, and some of them are even honest enough to admit it."

The Pro-Choice Movement Practices Its Own Form of Domestic Terrorism

Brian Clowes

In the following viewpoint, Brian Clowes states that any three-year-old child knows that an unborn child is a living human person. Pro-choice advocates, he writes, bend over backwards and twist themselves into knots in order to falsely argue that the fetus is not a living child. According to Clowes, "pro-abortion" advocates attempt to stifle pro-life freedom of choice by claiming that pro-life rhetoric leads to violence. Instead, it is the pro-choice movement that advocates violence against conservatives. But pro-lifers must not be intimidated by such tactics; they must advocate for the unborn until abortion is completely stopped. Brian Clowes is the director of education and research at Human Life International. He is a graduate of West Point and a member of the Army Special Forces ("Green Berets"). He is the author of as author of the pro-life informational resource volume The Facts of Life.

"Does Pro-Life Rhetoric Lead to Violence?" by Brian Clowes, Human Life International, June 7, 2017. Reprinted with permission of Human Life International at hli.org.

As you read, consider the following questions:

1. Why does the author call the opposition "pro-abortion" and "antilifers"?
2. How do pro-choicers themselves advocate violence, according to the viewpoint?
3. What is the difference between forceful pro-life and pro-choice speech according to the author?

Pro-abortionists frequently tell us to keep our opinions—and even our science—to ourselves. They say that we must not refer to abortionists as "baby killers" and to abortion as "murder." "Catholics" for a Free Choice goes even further, claiming that anyone who says that preborn children are human beings encourages terrorism.[1]

Pro abortionists have gone to great lengths to soothe the public with a cascade of meaningless "feel-good" words specifically designed to numb people's consciences. They call the preborn child a "blob of tissue;" the abortionist is a "reproductive health provider;" and the abortion procedure itself is a "voluntary interruption of pregnancy" (VIP) or "just like removing a wart or fingernail clippings."

They naturally become angry when pro-lifers undo all of their hard work and point out what any three-year-old child knows: That the preborn child is a living human person. The pro-abortionist's only option is to distract people from basic embryology to some tangential subject. So they allege that "anti-choice rhetoric" leads to violence. As one example, Planned Parenthood tried to force Laurel Cablevision of Torrington, Connecticut, to give up its plans to show Dr. Bernard Nathanson's film "The Silent Scream" by complaining that it would "spur violence against women's health clinics."[2]

The "Religious" Coalition for Reproductive Choice (RCRC) claims, "The notion that human life or personhood begins at the moment of conception is the foundation of anti-choice language … Inflammatory rhetoric has been a barely concealed invitation to violence. Those who commit acts of violence are responsible for their own actions, but anti-abortion leaders know the power of their words to make violence thinkable to their followers."[3]

However, it seems that pro-abortionists do not really believe that violent words and images lead to more violence—otherwise they would refrain from using it themselves. There are hundreds of examples of pro-abortionists and other liberals advocating death and destruction for conservatives, but Planned Parenthood, as always, stands out.

In 2005, Planned Parenthood-Golden Gate produced an animated cartoon called "A Superhero for Choice," which you can still find on YouTube. The "hero" of the movie is Dianysis, a super-powered woman who flies around San Francisco murdering pro-life activists by blowing them up, drowning them, and decapitating them, and apparently having a wonderful time doing it. After eliminating all of the "anti-choicers," a smiling Dianysis chirps, "That's more like it! Open for business! Now everyone that needs low cost and confidential health care may enter freely, without intimidation or violence."

Apparently, "pro-choicers" are utterly immune to the concept of irony.

Planned Parenthood quickly removed the video from its website after a number of people pointed out that it could be damaging to the "pro-choice" cause—not because they disagreed with its content. And, of course, PP never disavowed the video or apologized for it.

The difference between forceful pro-life and pro-abortion speech is that pro-lifers are defining and condemning what the pro-abortionists do; in return, the pro-abortionists are depicting the killing of pro-lifers (and, in some cases, taking matters into their own hands). In 2009, Harlan Drake executed pro-lifer Jim Pouillon because of his photos of aborted preborn babies, and not only did pro-abortion groups refuse to condemn the murder, but dozens of pro-abortionists cheered and supported the killing, saying "He got what was coming to him!"[4]

Some pro-lifers have urged others to tone down the forceful rhetoric. But we must not fool ourselves into thinking that pro-abortionists would limit themselves to banning pro-life speech if they had the power. Abortion is a very lucrative business.

Much more importantly, however, pro-lifers must understand that abortion is gender feminism's most powerful ideological symbol. It represents "choice" and "freedom" to anti-lifers more vividly than any other issue. For some of the most extreme, it is even a sacrament.[5] As Carolyn Hax of the *Washington Post* wrote:

> The abortion right is being left undefended by its true champions—the women who owe not their lives, but their lifestyles to the convenience of legal abortion.... Abortion has validated a lifestyle that allowed room for irresponsibility.... Among its perks are extended travel, higher education, unbroken career paths, choosing a different father, limiting family size, and going out and getting drunk after work.[6]

This is why pro-abortionists absolutely will not compromise on it, and this is why its advocates and defenders ardently desire to prohibit all pro-life activity. As Faye Wattleton, former President of the Planned Parenthood Federation of America, has said, "We need to remove the abortion issue forever from the legislative arena. We need a universal recognition that our civil liberties are off limits to partisan debate!"[7]

Since it is so visible to the public, many pro-abortionists especially want to outlaw all pro-life street activity, including rescue missions, sidewalk counseling, picketing and even silent prayer.[8] Some would also like to ban all behind the scenes activities by pro lifers, including crisis pregnancy centers, adoption, pro-life legislation, all lobbying, organizing and education, and even talking to our friends about abortion because they say that this is, believe it or not, "spiritual battering!"[9]

Some pro-abortionists say that priests and ministers must never mention abortion in their homilies or celebrate Sanctity of Life Sunday. They say that bishops cannot exert control over their own property by banning pro abortion meetings. In fact, some allege that the Catholic Church cannot even refuse to donate money to pro-abortion groups such as UNICEF.[10]

Finally, while ignoring women who are suffering from the mental and emotional aftereffects of abortions, many "pro-choicers" condemn even pro life attempts to help women with programs such as Project Rachel. Incredibly, they even denounce pro lifers who offer money and other aid to pregnant women to help them through their pregnancies and beyond.[11]

In summary, these pro-abortion extremists allege, "If religious leaders sincerely want to deter the terrorists, they must disavow one premise … that there is no significant difference between the human life of the unborn and human life of the born human being."[12]

The pro-abortionists are terrified that the visibility of the pro-life movement will sway public opinion against them. For these extremists, it is all about keeping pro-lifers out of the public eye.

There is a simple and straightforward explanation for this extreme "pro-choice" sensitivity to any form of opposition. The pro-abortionists know full well that we are right—they are killing babies, their consciences are stinging over it, and some of them are even honest enough to admit it.

For example, abortionist Magda Denes said:

> I do think abortion is murder—of a very special and necessary sort. What else would one call the deliberate stilling of a life? And no physician involved with the procedure ever kids himself about that … legalistic distinctions among "homicide," "justified homicide," "self defense," and "murder" appear to me a semantic game. What difference does it make what we call it? Those who do it and those who witness its doing know that abortion is the stilling of a life.[13]

Novelist Norman Mailer seconded this view when he said, "I am perfectly willing to grant that life starts at conception. If a woman doesn't want to have a child, then I think it's her right to say no. But let's not pretend that it isn't a form of killing."[14]

Even Faye Wattleton said, "Abortion is killing, but the bottom line is that if you can't control your reproduction, you're not likely to be controlling anything else."[15]

Abortion mill workers know that they are assisting in the killing a baby as well, and do everything they can to shield aborting women from this fact. Abortion mill nurse Norma Eidelman said, "We tried to avoid the women seeing them [the fetuses]. They always wanted to know the sex, but we lied and said it was too early to tell. It's better for the women to think of the fetus as an 'it.'"[16]

Abortion mill worker Kathy Sparks confessed:

> Sometimes we lied. A girl might ask what her baby was like at a certain point in the pregnancy: "Was it a baby yet?" Even as early as 12 weeks a baby is totally formed, he has fingerprints, turns his head, fans his toes, feels pain. But we would say "It's not a baby yet. It's just tissue, like a clot."[17]

Pro-abortionists are not concerned about the truth; they simply want to stamp out all opposition to abortion because it is so powerfully symbolic to them. Despite injunctions, despite threats, and despite endless pro-abortion violence, pro-lifers must continue to loudly and clearly proclaim the truth in as many ways and as many venues as possible until the very last preborn child is safe.

Endnotes

1. "In Brief." Conscience, Spring/Summer 1995, page 57.

2. "RTL and Cable TV." National Right to Life News, September 5, 1985, page 6.

3. "Words of Choice: Countering Anti-Choice Rhetoric." Website of the `Religious' Coalition for Reproductive Choice, http://www.rcrc.org/pdf/Words_of_Choice.pdf, September 19, 2012.

4. See Human Life International's Abortion Violence Web site at http://www.abortionviolence.com, under "Owosso, Michigan" for the complete story of the Pouillon murder.

5. See, for example, Ginette Paris' book The Sacrament of Abortion (translated from French by Joanna Mott) [Dallas: Spring Publications], 1992.

6. Copy Editor Carolyn Hax of the Washington Post, quoted in Stephen Settle. "There's No Middle Ground." National Catholic Register, April 25, 1993, page 5.

7. Faye Wattleton, former President of the Planned Parenthood Federation of America (PPFA). "Reproductive Rights Are Fundamental Rights." The Humanist, January/February 1991, page 21.

8. Ellen Carton, New York executive director of the National Abortion Rights Action League (NARAL), quoted in "Gazette." Conscience, May/June 1988, page 17; Annie Lally Milhaven. "Fatherly Fanaticism." Conscience, July/August 1988, page 6 ; Ellen Carton, New York executive director of the National Abortion Rights Action League (NARAL), says that " … commotion outside a clinic increases stress and affects the performance of medical personnel." Quoted in "Gazette." Conscience, May/June 1988, page 17; Frances Kissling has said that "Protesting or praying outside women's health centers by cardinals and other church leaders, no matter how non violent it appears, offends and hurts women." Quoted in Cathleen Falsani. "Abortion Foes Gather to Pray: Cardinal Bernardin Leads Mass at Chicago Clinic." Daily Southtown, June 27, 1999, pages 1 and 10.

9. Mary Jean Wolch. "An Open Letter from a Catholic Birth Mother." Conscience, Autumn 1996, pages 25 to 28; "Gazette." Conscience, May/June 1988, page 17; Letter by Rev. E.L. O'Hickey, Conscience, May/June 1988, page 19.

10. Margaret Conway. "State Updates." Conscience, July/August 1989, pages 16 and 17; "In the News: Not in My Building, You Don't." Conscience, January/February 1991, page 22; "In Brief." Conscience, Spring/Summer 1995, page 57; Frances Kissling. "The Vatican's Cheap Shot at UNICEF." Conscience, Winter 1996/1997, pages 36 and 37.

11. Excerpts from Frances Kissling's input to Annie Lally Milhaven's book Inside Stories: 13 Valiant Women Challenging the Church. Conscience, September/ December 1987, pages 29 to 37; Various pro abortionists, interviewed by Lisa M. Hisel and Patricia Miller. "Bribery or Benevolence: Prochoice Leaders Examine the Generosity of a Scottish Cardinal." Conscience, Winter 1999/2000.

12. "In Brief." Conscience, Spring/Summer 1995, page 57.

13. Magda Denes. "Performing Abortions." Commentary, October 1976, pages 33 to 37. This is a truly frightening and profoundly sickening article by a doctor who observes and describes in graphic detail a number of saline abortions and their results. She acknowledges that abortion is killing, but a type of "necessary" killing. Also see the "Letters" sections in the December 1976 and February 1977 issues of Commentary.

14. Norman Mailer on the David Frost Show. Quoted in "Norman Mailer Speaks Out on Sex and AIDS." American Family Association Journal, March 1992, page 3.

15. Faye Wattleton, former President of the Planned Parenthood Federation of America (PPFA), quoted in "Late-Term Abortion: Speaking Frankly." Ms. Magazine, May/June 1997, pages 67 to 71.

16. Abortion mill worker Norma Eidelman, quoted in James Tunstead Burtchaell [editor]. Rachel Weeping and Other Essays about Abortion [New York City: Universal Press], 1982 page 34.

17. Abortion mill worker Kathy Sparks, quoted in Gloria Williamson. "The Conversion of Kathy Sparks." Christian Herald, January 1986, page 28.

Periodical and Internet Sources Bibliography

The following articles have been selected to supplement the diverse views presented in this chapter.

Adriana Cohen, "Call Antifa what they are: domestic terrorists." *Boston Herald.com*, September 1, 2019. https://www. bostonherald.com/2019/09/01/call-antifa-what-they-are-domestic-terrorists/

David S. Cohen, "A Movement of None: The FBI's Bogus 'Pro-Choice Extremist' Label." Rewire.News, February 4, 2019. https://rewire. news/article/2019/02/04/a-movement-of-none-the-fbis-bogus-pro-choice-extremist-label/

Matt Ford, "The Danger of a Domestic Terrorism Law." *New Republic*, August 15, 2019. https://newrepublic.com/article/154785/danger-domestic-terrorism-law

David French, "It's Time to Declare War on White-Nationalist Terrorism." *National Review*, August 5, 2019. https://www. nationalreview.com/2019/08/declare-war-on-white-nationalist-terrorism/

Adam Goldman. "F.B.I., Pushing to Stop Domestic Terrorists, Grapples With Limits on Its Power." *New York Times*, June 4, 2019. https://www.nytimes.com/2019/06/04/us/politics/fbi-domestic-terrorism.html

Jeffrey C. Isaac, "Antifa Is Not a 'Terrorist Organization,' But That Doesn't Make Tt Good." Common Dreams, August 21, 2019. https://www.commondreams.org/views/2019/08/21/antifa-not-terrorist-organization-doesnt-make-it-good

Michael C. McGarrity, "Confronting the Rise of Domestic Terrorism in the Homeland." FBI.gov, May 8, 2009. https://www.fbi.gov/news/testimony/confronting-the-rise-of-domestic-terrorism-in-the-homeland

Harsha Panduranga and Faiza Patel, "'Domestic Terrorism' Bills Create More Problems Than they Solve." Just Security, August 28, 2019. https://www.justsecurity.org/65998/domestic-terrorism-bills-create-more-problems-than-they-solve/

Brian Pascus, What Is "Domestic Terrorism" and What Can the Law Do About It? CBS News, August 10, 2019. https://www.cbsnews.

com/news/what-is-domestic-terrorism-understanding-law-and-fbi-definitions-terrorist-activity-in-the-united-states/

Charlie Savage, "What Could a Domestic Terrorism Law Do?" *New York Times*, August 7, 2019. https://www.nytimes.com/2019/08/07/us/domestic-terror-law.html

Jessica Schulberg and Ryan J. Reilly, "Congress to Consider Domestic Terrorism Rule." Huffington Post, August 6, 2019. https://www.huffpost.com/entry/adam-schiff-domestic-terrorism-bill_n_5d56f7b8e4b0eb875f2383a1

OPPOSING
VIEWPOINTS®
SERIES

CHAPTER 2

Is Domestic Terrorism Ever Justified?

Chapter Preface

C an violence against one's country ever be justified? This is a thorny issue. Most people would immediately answer "No." The assumption is that only extreme radicals ever take matters into their own hands and use violence to threaten or intimidate their neighbors.

But many countries practice their own brand of domestic terrorism all of the time. Vladimir Putin's Russia routinely intimidates its own people, especially journalists and dissenters, through the threat of violence and incarceration. Saudi Arabia's Crown Prince Mohammad bin Salman ordered the assassination of journalist Jamal Khashoggi, who dared to speak out against the royal family. Violence against one's own people is a practice that comes right out of the authoritarian playbook.

China is another country that regularly intimidates its citizens. When the government crushed the Tiananmen Square protests of 1989, murdering hundreds to perhaps even thousands of its own peacefully protesting students and citizens (no one knows the exact figure), it was practicing a form of terrorism against its own people. But when state actors murder and intimidate, such actions are not typically referred to as terrorism. Historian Henry Commager observes that "Even when definitions of terrorism allow for *state terrorism*, state actions in this area tend to be seen through the prism of war or national self-defense, not terror."[1] Yet, he says, terrorism has been practiced by most of the world's great powers in the past century.

Is it morally unacceptable when citizens fight back? Certainly states believe so. They tend to label groups that rebel violently against unjust treatment as terrorists. Turkish strongman Recep Erdogan considers the ethnic group the Kurds to be terrorists, and has endeavored to wipe them out. Yet the Kurds have provided valuable assistance to the United States by fighting against ISIS, a true terrorist group that beheads innocent victims on internet videos. As the old saying goes, one person's terrorist is another's freedom fighter.

Take, for example, one instance of violence against a state by its people: the Hong Kong protests of 2019. Hong Kong was formerly a British colony. Under a nineteenth-century agreement with China, control of Hong Kong reverted to China in 1997. Since that time, the people of Hong Kong maintained their old freedoms despite being ruled by Communist China. The practice is called "one country, two systems." It is common knowledge, however, that China wants more control over Hong Kong. Hong Kong leaders, pressured by Chinese authorities, proposed a bill that would allow criminals and dissidents to be extradited to authoritarian China. This proposal provoked massive protests by the people of Hong Kong. Initially peaceful, the clashes grew violent as protesters clashed with the Hong Kong police. Though the extradition bill was subsequently withdrawn, the protests continued, as citizens feared the increasing influence of China on Hong Kong.

Are the Hong Kong protesters, who resorted to violence to counter the violence of the police, terrorists? Chinese authorities believe so. An October 2019 article in the *South China Post* bore this headline: "As Hong Kong protesters turn into terrorists, the city needs a comprehensive terrorism law."[2] The writer, Edward Chow, states that, "Undoubtedly, the violent protesters, by blocking the MTR [Mass Transit Railway], airport and highways, throwing petrol bombs, burning down Bank of China branches and damaging … restaurants and shops, fall within the definition of terrorists under the above law."[3]

It is unlikely that most impartial observers would claim that the Hong Kong protesters are domestic terrorists, but "terrorism" is clearly in the eye of the beholder. And branding a group with that label can do much to make their cause, however righteous, look sinister in the public eye.

Endnotes

1. Hor, Michael Yew Meng (2005). Global anti-terrorism law and policy. Cambridge University Press. p. 20.

2. "Edward Chow, As Hong Kong protesters turn into terrorists, the city needs a comprehensive terrorism law." South China Morning Post. October 21, 2019. https://www.scmp.com/comment/letters/article/3033589/hong-kong-protesters-turn-terrorists-city-needs-comprehensive

3. "Edward Chow, As Hong Kong protesters turn into terrorists, the city needs a comprehensive terrorism law." South China Morning Post. October 21, 2019. https://www.scmp.com/comment/letters/article/3033589/hong-kong-protesters-turn-terrorists-city-needs-comprehensive

"So, what we can say is that if we agree with the aims of a group, then violence is an ethically acceptable extension of the struggle; and if we disagree, it is not."

Terrorism Can Be Justified

Brian Brivati

In the following viewpoint, Brian Brivati weighs in on the thorny topic of justifiable terrorism. He argues that, as there is "just" war and unjust war, there are also cases where domestic violence can be an effective means toward achieving freedom and equality. Such was the case in South Africa, where violent acts by the African National Congress were a necessary step toward ending apartheid. The state does not have a monopoly on violence, Brivati suggests, and when states use brutality to suppress their people, those who violently oppose them may be terrorists, but they are not necessarily in the wrong. Brian Brivati is professor of contemporary history at Kingston University in London, England, where he runs the human rights programs. His articles have appeared in such British publications as the Guardian, *the* Financial Times, *the* Observer, *and the* New Statesman.

"Yes, Terrorism Can Be Justified," by Brian Brivati, Guardian News and Media Limited, August 19, 2009. Reprinted by permission.

As you read, consider the following questions:

1. Does the state alone have the right to commit violent acts against its people or can people fight back?
2. How was anti-apartheid violence in South Africa used as a means toward an end?
3. According to the viewpoint, what is the difference between terrorism and murder?

The presumption of critics of David Miliband's view that terrorism can be justified is, Natalie Hanman points out, that the state has a monopoly on violence, which therefore legitimates the use of it, and that any other group using violence is illegitimate. If this were true, then, when Nelson Mandela dies, he should be universally condemned as nothing more than a terrorist and murderer—something the Thatcher government liked to call him. This is not a serious position to hold.

Alternatively, we might say that the violence employed by all states, at least if they are western democracies, is illegitimate. Again, the many cases of the necessity of war—September 1939, for example—invalidate this position. So, what we can say is that if we agree with the aims of a group, then violence is an ethically acceptable extension of the struggle; and if we disagree, it is not.

These judgments need not be merely subjective but can be weighed up in the same way that any set of political actions are weighed up. While we may not reach an objective basis for the support of the armed struggle in one context as against another, we can at least suggest principles that are reasonable and then defend those principles. But more than this, we are also therefore forced to accept that the use of violence against "soft targets" is terrorism in whatever cause it is employed; the difference is that we might support some causes and not others because we see them as morally virtuous or vicious.

It was on this basis, belief in the cause, that Miliband was defending the anti-apartheid activist Joe Slovo. The use of violence, whether by states or other groups, should be based on the same argument as that used to justify a declaration of war—"just war" theory.

But let us not pretend that the causes we believe in are not using terror to further their aims just because we believe in them, or that the use of terror is not central to the possibility that they will be successful. The choice of terms here is not between freedom fighter and terrorist but between murderer and terrorist—the former simply killing nihilistically because they are killing in a cause we do not believe in, and the latter using violence as part of an achievable and just political project with which we agree.

Miliband's critics say that his justification for the ANC's armed struggle is giving comfort to the enemy in Afghanistan. How does this fit that case?

The Taliban are not merely a tribal group set on removing foreign invaders from their land; they have run a murderous state that sponsored war against other states, and now they make war on their own people to recreate that state with all the human rights violations they previously employed. They have a political strategy, but it is not more realistic than that of their allies in al-Qaida. I can understand how you could construct an argument that makes their use of violence legitimate, but I reject it.

The ANC, though, was also a terrorist group (through its military wing, Umkonto we Sizwe). So how can we decide between these groups? The difference is that the ANC deployed terror for the political purpose of destroying an obscene system that would not have been defeated otherwise. The economic boycott was important, but would the world have launched the boycott without the armed struggle? Would the people repressed under the apartheid police state have kept faith with the ANC if there had not been a dimension of armed resistance to the struggle? I doubt it very much.

Terrorism Can Never Be Justified

Nearly 200 people—representing all continents, as well as international organizations, research institutes and civil society—spent three days in the Tunisian capital, from 15 to 17 November, in discussions on a series of terrorism-related issues, including an examination of conditions conducive to terrorism, promoting education to prevent the phenomenon, encouraging greater inter-faith dialogue and the role of international and specialized organizations.

The conference, called Terrorism: Dimensions, Threats and Countermeasures, was jointly organized by the UN's Department of Political Affairs in collaboration with the Organization of the Islamic Conference (OIC) and its Islamic Educational, Scientific and Cultural Organization (ISESCO). It was hosted by the Tunisian Government and held under the high patronage of Zine El Abidine Ben Ali, President of Tunisia.

In the official concluding observations Saturday, a co-chair, Tunisian Culture and Preservation of Heritage Minister Mohamed El Aziz Ben Achour, said the prevailing view of participants "was that terrorism and extremism constitute a threat to the peace, security and stability of all countries and peoples."

He added: "Terrorism has no justification, no matter what pretext terrorists may use for their deeds."

In the case of the Taliban, the strategy is to regain and hold power through terror, and run a state based on the suppression of human rights and the sponsorship of international terrorist attacks against civilian targets. The means and the ends of the Taliban's cause strike me as the opposite of just, and are entirely illegitimate. But each of these groups can correctly be called terrorist and should be referred to as such—but that is where the analysis should begin, not end.

What were, or are, they each fighting for? Or against? How do they use terror? Who are their targets? What is their political strategy? These are the questions that need to be asked. In assessing

Participants agreed that terrorism flourishes in environments where there is discontent, exclusion, humiliation, poverty, political oppression and human rights abuses, as well as in countries engaged in regional conflicts.

"It profits from weak State capacity to maintain law and order," Mr. Ben Achour said. "These vulnerable areas are exploited by terrorists to mobilize recruits and justify violence. None of the religions are a cause of political radicalism and extremism. Religious doctrine may be 'tools of mobilization,' rather than a direct cause."

The participants said it was important for the international community to counter the spread of Islamophobia, which it noted has been growing in recent years in part because of misinformation and misperceptions about the religion.

"The emergence of misguided groups that have deviated from the straight path to fanaticism, violence and extremism, attributing their acts to Islam, in no way justifies associating this phenomenon with the Islamic faith. True Islam is the religion of moderation and avoidance of excess, founded on the values of equality, justice, peace and brotherhood."

"Terrorism Can Never Be Justified, Participants at Joint UN Conference Conclude," United Nations, November 19, 2007.

a campaigner's life, as Miliband was doing, you have to look at the broad picture.

When the Maquis, for instance, were killing German troops and when the Warsaw Ghetto rose up, they killed every enemy they could find. They wanted to hurl some of the terror that they had faced back in the faces of their oppressors. Were they terrorists—in the sense that they used terror to further their cause? Yes, they were. But their cause was just and their violence justifiable. When the Nazis who survived formed the Werwolf resistance groups and attacked the occupying allied forces, were they terrorists? Yes, they were. But the end they fought for was obscene and so they also deserved to be called murderers. It is not the term itself that matters, but the cause for which the violence is used that should concern us.

Will the troops in Afghanistan be demoralised by Miliband's defence of the armed struggle against apartheid? I doubt it very much. Members of the British armed forces, in my experience, have a lot more political sense than many of the politicians who choose to speak for them.

> *"Attempting to turn activism into terrorism is not a new trick. In the 1980s, the FBI used unsubstantiated allegations of material support for terrorism to investigate, harass, and intimidate those working to change US foreign policy in Central America."*

Activism Is Not Terrorism

Defending Rights & Dissent

In the following viewpoint authors from Defending Rights & Dissent attempt to differentiate between activism and terrorism, citing incidents where the US government has used deceptive means and trickery to subvert legitimate protest. The viewpoint cites two prominent examples of such federal dirty tricks: the Palmer Raids during the first Red Scare in the United States and Cointelpro, which attempted to discredit left-leaning groups. In recent cases the FBI and the Department of Homeland Security have used counterterrorism tactics to target Occupy Wall Street, Black Lives Matter, and anti-Keystone XL Pipeline activists. This is clearly wrong, according to the author, as these are not terrorist organizations. Unfortunately, the viewpoint concludes, such tactics are likely to continue. Defending Rights & Dissent is a national not-for-profit advocacy organization focused on defending participatory democracy by protecting the right to political expression.

"Activism Is Not Terrorism," Defending Rights & Dissent. Reprinted by permission.

As you read, consider the following questions:

1. According to the authors, how has the US government used "dirty tricks" against legitimate protestors and activists?
2. What is the mission of the organization behind this viewpoint?
3. Why does the viewpoint suggest that the government's dirty tricks are likely to continue?

It is no secret that the state has tried to thwart activists for decades. From the Palmer Raids to COINTELPRO to the corralling of demonstrators into so-called "free speech zones" the state has quite the bag of dirty tricks. One of the state's favorite tricks is conflating activism with terrorism.

Attempting to turn activism into terrorism is not a new trick. In the 1980s, the FBI used unsubstantiated allegations of material support for terrorism to investigate, harass, and intimidate those working to change US foreign policy in Central America. Starting in the early 1990s, the FBI and others started clamoring about "eco-terrorism," a label often applied to non-violent civil disobedience. In this century the FBI used "domestic terrorism" as an excuse to investigate non-violent civil disobedience committed by pacifists and the material support for terrorism statute to raid the homes of anti-war activists.

The Activism is Not Terrorism campaign focuses on protecting the rights of activists with an emphasis on the increased use of anti-terrorism legislation against non-violent activists, terrorism as a pretext for the surveillance of First Amendment protected activities, and attempts to limit the First Amendment rights of protestors at public events like national political conventions.

Investigate the FBI

While the issue of mass surveillance by the NSA and FBI has received considerable attention, the continued targeted surveillance of political activist groups has not. After the outrage of COINTELPRO was exposed, reforms were adopted to limit the FBI's ability to engage in political spying. Those reforms were short-lived, and the FBI quickly found new authorities under which to conduct their political spying: counterterrorism.

In the 1980s, the FBI used unsubstantiated allegations of material support for terrorism to investigate, harass, and intimidate those working to change US foreign policy in Central America. Starting in the early 1990s, the FBI and others started clamoring about "eco-terrorism," a label often applied to non-violent civil disobedience. In this century the FBI used "domestic terrorism" as an excuse to investigate non-violent civil disobedience committed by pacifists and the material support for terrorism statute to raid the homes of anti-war activists.

The FBI's capacity to monitor innocent people in the United States has steadily expanded, particularly in the post 9/11 era. Technological advances combined with new authorities and relaxed rules found in the PATRIOT Act, the FISA Amendments Act and new, less restrictive Attorney General Guidelines have been a boon to surveillance. So has the expansion of agency personnel. The FBI has a network of 15,000 paid informants at 15,000, a tenfold increase over the number reportedly active during COINTELPRO. The FBI budget is $8.3 billion, the agency employs 35,000 people, including 13,000 agents and 300 intelligence analysts. In 1970, the budget was $257 million, there were 7,600 FBI agents, and no category of 'intelligence analyst.'

The targets of surveillance and infiltration have often been peaceful political groups. In 2010, the DOJ Inspector General issued a scathing report on the FBI's inappropriate monitoring of six different political groups including Greenpeace, PETA, and the Thomas Merton Center from 2001 through 2006. More recently, the FBI, the Department of Homeland Security have used counterterrorism authorities to target the School of the Americas Watch(SOAW), Occupy Wall Street, Black Lives Matter, and anti-Keystone XL Pipeline activists.

Animal Rights and Environmentalism

Defending Rights & Dissent is building a coalition of national and local organizations to repeal the Animal Enterprise Terrorism Act (AETA), one of the most blatant examples of Congress expanding the definition of terrorism to crush powerful social movements.

At the state level, we are monitoring Ag-Gag legislation, laws that are aimed at preventing whistleblowers from exposing poor treatment of animals at factory farms or meat processing plants. Generally, the laws make it a crime to lie on a job application and/or to take pictures or film at an agriculture facility. In 2015, Ag-Gag laws were expanded in two states: in North Carolina, every industry is covered, including nursing homes and day care providers; Wyoming's law criminalizes taking water samples in public waterways.

Both AETA and ag-gag have undergone an escalation in recent years. In spite of years of dormancy federal prosecutors have pursued AETA indictments twice in the last year. Twenty-two states have considered ag-gag laws since 2012.

Activism is being equated with terrorism with deleterious effects on the First Amendment rights of all Americans.

National Political Conventions

Elections are supposed to be the hallmark of American democracy and every electoral season includes political conventions. Yet, instead of embodying the spirit of democracy conventions are tightly controlled made-for-TV spectacles that trample on dissent. Political protestors from nearly every cause, from anti-death penalty and anti-war to AIDS awareness, make their way to conventions to protest in the streets outside. Hosting cities, however, often over react to such protests.

Trampling of dissent at conventions is quite the norm. The police violence against protestors at the 1968 Chicago Democratic National Convention has come to symbolize in American history the violent repression of protests. But suppression of dissent at conventions did not end in Chicago.

- During the 2000 Los Angeles Democratic Convention, the city consistently tried to prevent Rage Against the Machine from playing a concert in protest against the two-party system. A federal judge forced the city to allow Rage Against the Machine to hold its concert across the street from the DNC. The night ended with police attacking protesters with rubber bullets and pepper spray as Hillary and Bill Clinton spoke inside.
- Things were not much better in 2000 in Philadelphia, where the Republican Convention was held. Police infiltrated protest groups and even raided a warehouse containing puppets made by the protesters. Per the police affidavit supporting the puppet raid police were concerned that activists were being funded by "communists" and even international trade union with ties to the "former Soviet union."
- The 2004 New York Republican National Convention holds the record for number of protesters arrested—1,800. However, 90% of those arrested had their charges dropped.
- Before the 2008 St. Paul Republican Convention police raided an anarchist group, "RNC Welcoming Committee." Eight individuals associated with the RNC Welcoming Committee were arrested and charged with "conspiracy to riot in furtherance of terrorism." Setting the tone for what would come; during the first three days of the convention 300 people were arrested. Among those arrested were several journalists, including Amy Goodman—who latter successfully sued the city.

These are, of course, not the only examples of political repression at political conventions. Sadly, if history is any indicator of the future we can expect political oppression to accompany the 2016 Democratic and Republican National Conventions in Philadelphia and Cleveland.

> *"Civilian and government agents are on a par, and we have identical rights of self-defence (and defence of others) against both. We should presume, by default, that government agents have no special immunity against self-defence ...."*

Violence Against Unjust Government Agents Is Justified

Jason Brennan

In the following viewpoint Jason Brennan asserts that self-defense, including violence, against the police or government agents can be justified under certain circumstances. Americans have long applauded passive resistance, he writes, but violence is a less appreciated response to oppression. Unfortunately, Brennon writes, peaceful opposition is not always effective. While violence against oppression should not be one's first impulse, true change rarely occurs through peaceful methods alone. Jason Brennan is professor of strategy, economics, ethics and public policy at Georgetown University. His books include Markets Without Limits *and* When All Else Fails: The Ethics of Resistance to State Injustice.

As you read, consider the following questions:

1. Why are average citizens so loathe to confront authorities who misuse their positions of power?
2. In what types of situations does the author advocate a physical or violent response to authority?
3. How does the author subvert the common notion that Martin Luther King established his goals through non-violence alone?

If you see police choking someone to death—such as Eric Garner, the 43-year-old black horticulturalist wrestled down on the streets of New York City in 2014—you might choose to pepper-spray them and flee. You might even save an innocent life. But what ethical considerations justify such dangerous heroics? (After all, the cops might arrest or kill you.) More important: do we have the right to defend ourselves and others from government injustice when government agents are following an unjust law? I think the answer is yes. But that view needs defending. Under what circumstances might active self-defence, including possible violence, be justified, as opposed to the passive resistance of civil disobedience that Americans generally applaud?

Civil disobedience is a public act that aims to create social or legal change. Think of Henry David Thoreau's arrest in 1846 for refusing to pay taxes to fund the colonial exploits of the United States, or Martin Luther King Jr courting the ire of the authorities in 1963 to shame white America into respecting black civil rights. In such cases, disobedient citizens visibly break the law and accept punishment, so as to draw attention to a cause. But justifiable resistance need not have a civic character. It need not aim at changing the law, reforming dysfunctional institutions or replacing bad leaders. Sometimes, it is simply about stopping an immediate injustice. If you stop a mugging, you are trying to stop that mugging in that moment, not trying to end muggings everywhere. Indeed, had you pepper-sprayed the police officer Daniel Pantaleo while he choked Eric Garner, you'd have been trying to save Garner, not reform US policing.

Generally, we agree that it's wrong to lie, cheat, steal, deceive, manipulate, destroy property or attack people. But few of us think that the prohibitions against such actions are absolute. Commonsense morality holds that such actions are permissible in self-defence or in defence of others (even if the law doesn't always agree). You may lie to the murderer at the door. You may smash the windows of the would-be kidnapper's car. You may kill the would-be rapist.

Here's a philosophical exercise. Imagine a situation in which a civilian commits an injustice, the kind against which you believe it is permissible to use deception, subterfuge or violence to defend yourself or others. For instance, imagine your friend makes an improper stop at a red light, and his dad, in anger, yanks him out of the car, beats the hell out of him, and continues to strike the back of his skull even after your friend lies subdued and prostrate. May you use violence, if it's necessary to stop the father? Now imagine the same scene, except this time the attacker is a police officer in Ohio, and the victim is Richard Hubbard III, who in 2017 experienced just such an attack as described. Does that change things? Must you let the police officer possibly kill Hubbard rather than intervene?

Most people answer yes, believing that we are forbidden from stopping government agents who violate our rights. I find this puzzling. On this view, my neighbours can eliminate our right of self-defence and our rights to defend others by granting someone an office or passing a bad law. On this view, our rights to life, liberty, due process and security of person can disappear by political fiat— or even when a cop has a bad day. In *When All Else Fails: The Ethics of Resistance to State Injustice* (2019), I argue instead that we may act defensively against government agents under the same conditions in which we may act defensively against civilians. In my view, civilian and government agents are on a par, and we have identical rights of self-defence (and defence of others) against both. We should presume, by default, that government agents have no special immunity against self-defence, unless we can discover good reason to think otherwise. But it turns out that the leading arguments for special immunity are weak.

Some people say we may not defend ourselves against government injustice because governments and their agents have "authority." (By definition, a government has authority over you if, and only if, it can oblige you to obey by fiat: you have to do what it says because it says so.) But the authority argument doesn't work. It's one thing to say that you have a duty to pay your taxes, show up for jury duty, or follow the speed limit. It is quite another to show that you are specifically bound to allow a government and its agents to use excessive violence and ignore your rights to due process. A central idea in liberalism is that whatever authority governments have is limited.

Others say that we should resist government injustice, but only through peaceful methods. Indeed, we should, but that doesn't differentiate between self-defence against civilians or government. The common-law doctrine of self-defence is always governed by a necessity proviso: you may lie or use violence only if necessary, that is, only if peaceful actions are not as effective. But peaceful methods often fail to stop wrongdoing. Eric Garner peacefully complained: "I can't breathe," until he drew his last breath.

Another argument is that we shouldn't act as vigilantes. But invoking this point here misunderstands the antivigilante principle, which says that when there exists a workable public system of justice, you should defer to public agents trying, in good faith, to administer justice. So if cops attempt to stop a mugging, you shouldn't insert yourself. But if they ignore or can't stop a mugging, you may intervene. If the police themselves are the muggers— as in unjust civil forfeiture—the antivigilante principle does not forbid you from defending yourself. It insists you defer to more competent government agents when they administer justice, not that you must let them commit injustice.

Some people find my thesis too dangerous. They claim that it's hard to know exactly when self-defence is justified; that people make mistakes, resisting when they should not. Perhaps. But that's true of self-defence against civilians, too. No one says we lack a right of self-defence against each other because applying the principle is hard. Rather, some moral principles are hard to apply.

However, this objection gets the problem exactly backwards. In real life, people are too deferential and conformist in the face of government authority. They are all-too-willing to electrocute experimental subjects, gas Jews or bomb civilians when ordered to, and reluctant to stand up to political injustice. If anything, the dangerous thesis—the thesis that most people will mistakenly misapply—is that we should defer to government agents when they seem to act unjustly. Remember, self-defence against the state is about stopping an immediate injustice, not fixing broken rules.

Of course, strategic nonviolence is usually the most effective way to induce lasting social change. But we should not assume that strategic nonviolence of the sort that King practised always works alone. Two recent books—Charles Cobb Jr's *This Nonviolent Stuff'll Get You Killed* (2014) and Akinyele Omowale Umoja's *We Will Shoot Back* (2013)—show that the later 'nonviolent' phase of US civil rights activism succeeded (in so far as it has) only because, in earlier phases, black people armed themselves and shot back in self-defence. Once murderous mobs and white police learned that black people would fight back, they turned to less violent forms of oppression, and black people in turn began using nonviolent tactics. Defensive subterfuge, deceit and violence are rarely first resorts, but that doesn't mean they are never justified.

VIEWPOINT 4

> *"The anti-abortion movement does not promote life; it promotes lies. It does not show compassion; it shows contempt. But their hate is no match for this powerful truth, originally stated by reproductive justice activist Renee Bracey Sherman: 'Everyone loves someone who has had an abortion.'"*

Anti-Abortion Violence Is Unacceptable

Jill Heaviside and Rosann Mariappuram

In the following viewpoint, Jill Heaviside and Rosann Mariappuram argue that violence is a hallmark of the pro-life movement. The authors cite famous instances of pro-life violence and murder to support their case. They assert that the anti-abortion movement is an angry, dangerous minority that seeks to exert power of those who exercise their right to reproductive freedom. Their violence is never acceptable, the authors contend, and must be rejected. Jill Heaviside is a lawyer and Reproductive Justice Fellow with SisterLove, Inc. in Atlanta Georgia. Rosann Mariappuram is a lawyer and Reproductive Justice Fellow with Surge Reproductive Justice and Legal Voice in Seattle, Washington.

"The Escalation of Anti-Abortion Violence Ten Years After Dr. George Tiller's Murder," by Jill Heaviside and Rosann Mariappuram, Rewire.News, May 31, 2019. Reprinted by permission.

As you read, consider the following questions:

1. Why do the authors take exception to Senator Ben Sasse's implication that the pro-life movement has never been violent?
2. What incidents do the authors cite to dispute Sasse?
3. According to the viewpoint, what is the real aim of anti-abortion groups?

As we mark the tenth anniversary of the assassination of Dr. George Tiller, it is incredible to think that, just over a month ago, Republican Sen. Ben Sasse was really asking how "the pro-life position is in any way violent."

Violence has been a central tenet of the anti-abortion movement since before the US Supreme Court decided *Roe v. Wade.* As activists have sought control over the reproductive freedom of millions of people—particularly women of color, low-income women and families, and queer, gender-nonconforming, and transgender communities—they have used violence as a tactic of control, abuse, and fear across the United States.

Dr. Tiller was Wichita's only abortion provider for 40 years and was known for his deep commitment to trusting women and their families' reproductive health decisions. Because of his work, Dr. Tiller was a target of many anti-abortion groups; before he was killed, he survived a clinic bombing and a prior shooting.

Dr. Tiller's murder wasn't an isolated incident. Anti-abortion extremists have killed at least 11 people since the 1990s. Their violent history includes the first recorded murder of an abortion provider, Dr. David Gunn, in 1993, and the 2015 shooting at a Planned Parenthood clinic in Colorado Springs, which claimed three lives and injured nine people.

For every reported murder, there have been countless credible threats of violence against abortion providers and instances of arson, burglary, and vandalism against health clinics. Some are isolated events but others are part of highly organized and premeditated showings of force that seek to intimidate providers and deter people from seeking care.

Violence is not just in the anti-abortion movement's past. The National Abortion Federation (NAF), which tracks these incidents, found in its latest report record numbers of violent and disruptive incidents at clinics in 2018. NAF recorded the greatest number of trespassing incidents since the organization began tracking in 1999, and the incidents of obstruction of health-care facilities doubled from 2017 to 2018.

In addition to violence against abortion providers and incursions onto physical clinic property, staff and volunteers are subject to violence. In 2015, Calla Hales, director of A Preferred Women's Health Center (APWHC) in North Carolina, was sexually assaulted by a person who targeted her because of her work. And earlier this year, Helmi Henkin, chair of the West Alabama Clinic Defenders, saw an increase in protester aggression, culminating with an anti-abortion activist backing into a clinic escort with his car.

This recent escalation in violence mirrors the increasingly extreme restrictions on abortion seen in statehouses across the country. Twenty-eight states introduced bills that would ban abortion in some way in the first few months of 2019. Alabama passed a total abortion ban—without exception for rape or incest— that carries a penalty of up to 99 years in prison for doctors who provide an abortion. In Texas, legislators introduced a restriction that could subject people to the death penalty for having an abortion. And today, on the anniversary of Dr. Tiller's assassination, the fate of Missouri's last remaining abortion provider is still unknown. While the clinic will not be forced to stop providing abortion services tonight, if its license is not renewed, Missouri will become the first state to not offer safe, legal abortion services since the right to abortion was established in 1973.

While reproductive health, rights, and justice advocates are relentlessly challenging these bills in court, this administration has stacked the judicial branch with anti-abortion judges, many of whom prioritize politics over precedent. Just this week, the Supreme Court upheld an Indiana law—signed by then-Gov. Mike Pence—requiring fetal remains to be buried or cremated. In a 20-page concurrence, Justice Clarence Thomas compared abortion and certain forms of birth control to racial eugenics and stated that the Court will need to consider the constitutionality of abortion laws soon.

It's not surprising to see that policies once considered too severe by opponents to abortion rights are now woven into the mainstream anti-abortion framework, especially considering that these activists, legislators, and judges have been emboldened by our current president. In March 2016, then-candidate Donald Trump said that there had to be "some form of punishment" for people seeking abortion. Since then, he has continued to perpetuate dangerous myths about abortion, claiming that "babies are ripped from their mother's womb moments before birth" during the 2019 State of the Union and that parents and doctors conspire to commit infanticide shortly after birth. None of these statements are grounded in fact but they serve to drive anti-abortion fervor and incite violence across the country.

Despite legislators' frequent claims that abortion restrictions do not target patients, people like Kasey Dischman, Kenlissa Jones, and Purvi Patel have been charged or imprisoned for their pregnancy outcomes and, just this month, conservative writers called the failure to prosecute women who end their pregnancies "a miscarriage of justice." Some prosecutors have gone further and have made their intentions known. In Georgia, after a group of district attorneys pledged to not prosecute women under the state's new six-week abortion ban, another doubled down, stating, "Women need to be made aware. The only way to be 100 percent sure you're not prosecuted is not to have an abortion."

It makes sense. The movement to ban abortion has always been about the control and punishment of pregnant people, but until recently, most anti-abortion lobby groups, politicians, and activists have been reluctant to admit the obvious: That outlawing abortion necessitates the policing of pregnancy and the investigation and prosecution of pregnant people.

The anti-abortion movement does not promote life; it promotes lies. It does not show compassion; it shows contempt. But their hate is no match for this powerful truth, originally stated by reproductive justice activist Renee Bracey Sherman: "Everyone loves someone who has had an abortion."

Abortion providers like Dr. Tiller dedicate their lives to trusting pregnant people to make their own decisions: The Trust Women Foundation was founded in his honor and continues to carry out his mission.

It's past time to call the anti-abortion movement what it is: an angry, dangerous minority that seeks to maintain power at the expense of the health and safety of millions of people in the United States. We should all reject it as such—for Dr. Tiller's memory and for our future.

> *"These core American beliefs all point to the same commitment: that civic resistance is sometimes justified, and that those who oppose injustice and tyranny are sometimes permitted violence in self-defence."*

Justifying Violent Protest

Christopher J. Finlay

In the following viewpoint Christopher J. Finlay asks whether violent actions are ever justified as a means of political protest. The author defines violence as "the intentional infliction of physical harm against people or property." Such violence can backfire, he writes, as it may mobilize public opinion against protesters or be met by escalating government violence. But to claim that violence is never permissible is also going too far. Individuals have the right to resist and rebel against tyrannical government and political injustices; defeating evil may sometimes demand armed resistance. But if violence is used, those who do so must be prepared to defend their actions against the inevitable misrepresentation of their deeds. Christopher J. Finlay is a professor in political theory at Durham University, England. He is the author of Terrorism and the Right to Resist: a Theory of Just Revolutionary War.

As you read, consider the following questions:

1. When, according to the author, is armed violence a permissible form of resistance to goverments?
2. How does the second amendment provide for armed protest against a tyrannical government, according to some mentioned in the viewpoint?
3. How might violent political protest against Donald Trump backfire, according to the author?

The mass protests against Donald Trump's election, inauguration, and executive actions might subside—but based on the scale and intensity of what's already happened, there's probably more to come.

So far, most protesters have limited themselves to marching, placard-waving, and other "peaceful" methods. There has, however, been some violence, and some demonstrators have adopted "disruptive" methods that fall somewhere between the purely peaceful and clearly violent. Obstructing access to airport terminals or blocking highways, for instance, needn't involve violence, but such tactics can all too easily be reframed in ways that can turn public attitudes against them. This in turn could help legitimise legal sanctions against protesters.

Because disruptive methods are ambiguous and vulnerable to political manipulation, difficult questions are never far away—and one of the thorniest is the question of what the word "violence" actually refers to.

Many political thinkers have argued over the respective merits of narrow definitions (where "violence" is chiefly seen as physical attack) and wider ones (encompassing indirect, unintended harm). Given that today's conscientious protesters face the risk that disruptive but nonviolent methods might be recategorised as violent security threats or their equivalent, a clear, narrow definition of violence is probably the safest for their purposes.

But there's another question to answer: even if violence is defined as the intentional infliction of physical harm against people or property, is it always absolutely unacceptable for protesters to commit acts of violence?

The Fine Line

For current protester leaders to encourage violence would be both morally unjustified and a serious tactical mistake. The outcome of any struggle between them and the government will be decided in large part by public opinion: if protesters can be blamed for starting violence, that will elevate the administration and its supporters. And worse yet, it might also help legitimise harsher methods by the security forces in response.

But it's also a mistake to overstate the case against violence. For one thing, the claim that violence is never permissible under any circumstances probably isn't true—at least not if you're committed to the sort of liberal, republican, and democratic ideas that the US's founding fathers believed in. Modern democratic thought has long held that individuals have a right to resist and rebel against tyrannical government and political injustices, and that defeating these great social evils may sometimes demand the resort to armed force. Properly understood, these sorts of ethics are highly restrictive: it's probably not justifiable for opponents of injustice to instigate violence. But if the defenders of an unjust government take the initiative, using violence as a means of deterring protest, that is a different matter.

As the English-American revolutionary Thomas Paine wrote in his 1776 pamphlet *Common Sense*, when struggling to defend rights against tyranny, "it is the violence which is done and threatened to our persons … which conscientiously qualifies the use of arms".

This view of armed resistance still finds plenty of support across the spectrum of the US's political culture, though it's more frequently cited on the political right than on the left. And its roots date back right to the start of the American project.

ARE ANIMAL RIGHTS ACTIVISTS TERRORISTS?

Animal rights activists who invade farms to stage protests will be hit with huge new fines in measures announced by Australia's southeastern state government after they were branded "domestic terrorists" by the region's deputy leader.

The New South Wales (NSW) government has introduced on-the-spot trespassing charges of $1,000 (£565) for each "vigilante" caught illegally entering private farmland.

The new rules, which come into force on 1 August, could also see individuals charged up to $220,000 (£124,000) and corporations up to $440,000 (£248,000) for any major violations of the Biosecurity Act.

"Vigilantes who are entering our farmers' property illegally are nothing short of domestic terrorists," said NSW deputy premier John Barilaro, in remarks widely reported by Australian media.

"Our farmers have had a gutful. They don't deserve, nor have time, to be dealing with illegal trespass and vile harassment from a bunch of virtue-signalling thugs."

The penalties follows a series of demonstrations and direct action staged by vegan activists at private farms and abattoirs in recent months.

Earlier this year clashes between farm owners and protesters forced the police to step in Western Australia, and the owners of a

The right to resist tyranny and grave injustice was well understood by the 18th-century American revolutionaries, who drew inspiration from John Locke's Second Treatise of Government, published in 1689. Locke argued that if rulers exceeded their constitutional authority, the people would in principle be justified if they resorted to armed revolt. And when he drafted the American Declaration of Independence, Thomas Jefferson treated this idea as "self-evident".

And then there's the US Constitution's Second Amendment. Nowadays, the "right to keep and bear arms" that the amendment enshrines is most often defended by right-wingers, but it originated small goat farm in Victoria blamed closure on continual harassment by abusive "vegan activists."

Officials are also considering "jail time" as additional punishment. "Today the government is putting these vigilantes and thugs on notice," said NWS agriculture minister Adam Marshall, Australia's ABC News reported.

"This is just the first part of a broader package of reforms the government is working on, and jail time will be included in further legislation we are looking at."

He also claimed the new rules were "the toughest laws anywhere in Australia for people that illegally trespass onto farmers' properties."

Prime minister Scott Morrison recently pledged to introduced national legislation to crack down on animal rights activists invading private properties.

The campaign group Aussie Farms claimed the new fines introduced by the NWS government under the "smokescreen" of biosecurity were heavy-handed.

"Once again, the issue of biosecurity is being used as an excuse to attempt to limit consumer awareness of the systemic cruelty occurring in farms and slaughterhouses across the country," said executive director Chris Delforce.

**"Animal Rights Activists Designated 'Domestic Terrorists' in Australia,"
The Independent.**

in 18th-century debates about the danger to the republic posed by permitting the state to monopolise the means of violence through the creation of a standing army. Proponents of the right to bear arms believed that a citizen militia would be a better bulwark against both foreign enemies and would-be tyrants within.

Another view widely accepted in the US (especially among advocates of gun ownership) is that innocent victims of violent attacks have a right to defend themselves. Nowadays, this right is more often discussed in cases of home invasion or other types of crime. But as Paine thought, the right to self-defence must also apply to those peacefully resisting injustice: if they are threatened with wrongful violence, then they too have a moral right to self-defence.

These core American beliefs all point to the same commitment: that civic resistance is sometimes justified, and that those who oppose injustice and tyranny are sometimes permitted violence in self-defence. To be clear, this isn't the same as suggesting that protesters ought to resort to arms. But if the left too eagerly rejects the idea that armed resistance can ever be justified, its leaders and footsoldiers will be vulnerable on two fronts.

Own Goals

First, it's naive to imagine that protest leaders are always in total control. Violence sometimes happens whether they sanction it or not.

This was the argument Nelson Mandela made to justify the ANC's use of sabotage: given the intensity of popular anger and outrage in South Africa, he said, the question wasn't whether violence would occur, but how to limit and guide it. The US certainly isn't at that point yet, but at least some outbreaks of violence are inevitable, and they might get worse over time.

Second, when violence does occur, those who are most hostile to the protesters will inevitably describe it as a self-evident wrong, morally as well as legally. An indiscriminate rejection of popular violence by protest leaders will be matched by that of the security forces.

The political scientist Erica Chenoweth rightly argues that any violent outbreaks now could seriously undercut the moral case Trump's opponents are trying to make. But if advocates of civil resistance stick to the line that "justified violence" is a contradiction in terms, they will simply hand the other side an argument to be used against them.

If violence seems likely for whatever reason, the opposition needs to be able to defend its members against any misrepresentation of their intentions. Refusing to acknowledge even hypothetical justifications for violence gives up on a vital line of defence.

Periodical and Internet Sources Bibliography

The following articles have been selected to supplement the diverse views presented in this chapter.

Natasha Bach, "Domestic Terrorism Is on the Rise. But How Prepared Is the US to Counter It?" *Fortune*, April 4, 2019. https://fortune.com/2019/04/04/dhs-domestic-terrorism/

Grenville Cross, "Violent protest must end: Let's all defend the rule of law." Star Online, July 2, 2019. https://www.thestar.com.my/news/regional/2019/07/02/violent-protest-must-end-let-us-all-defend-the-rule-of-law

Darlena Cunha, "Ferguson: In Defense of Rioting." *Time,* November 25, 2014. https://time.com/3605606/ferguson-in-defense-of-rioting/

David Harsanyi, "There Is No 'Surge' in Right-Wing Violence." Real Clear Politics, November 30, 2018. https://www.realclearpolitics.com/articles/2018/11/30/there_is_no_surge_in_right-wing_violence_138791.html

Emily Johnston, "I shut down an oil pipeline—because climate change is a ticking bomb." *Guardian*, November 24, 2017. https://www.theguardian.com/commentisfree/2017/nov/24/oil-pipeline-valve-turner-protest-climate-change

Olga Khazan, "The Futility of Anti-Abortion Terrorism." *Atlantic*, December 2, 2015. https://www.theatlantic.com/politics/archive/2015/12/the-futility-of-anti-abortion-terrorism/418278/

Dan McLaughlin, "Why We Panic about Immigration." *National Review*, January 21, 2019. https://www.nationalreview.com/2019/01/immigration-why-we-panic-birth-rates-assimilation/

Michael E. Miller and Yanan Wang, "The radical, unrepentant ideology of abortion clinic killers." *Washington Post*, November 30, 2015. https://www.washingtonpost.com/news/morning-mix/wp/2015/11/30/the-radical-unrepentant-ideology-of-abortion-clinic-killers/

Dan Sanchez, "The Sniper Shooting in Dallas Was Both Murder and Blowback." Foundation for Economic Education, July 8, 2016.

https://fee.org/articles/the-sniper-shooting-in-dallas-was-both-murder-and-blowback

Anna Schecter, "The Feds Need to Up Their Game Against Domestic Extremists, Critics Say." NBC News, May 15, 2019. https://www.nbcnews.com/politics/justice-department/feds-need-their-game-against-domestic-extremists-say-critics-n1006001

Jamil Smith, Op-Ed: "Why would Charlottesville racists do so much to protect a Robert E. Lee statue?" *Los Angeles Times,* August 14, 2017. https://www.latimes.com/opinion/op-ed/la-oe-smith-charlottesville-statue-20170814-story.html

Abigail Tracy, "'The President of the United States Says It's Okay': The Rise of the Trump Defense." *Vanity Fair*, August 8, 2019. https://www.vanityfair.com/news/2019/08/donald-trump-domestic-terrorism-el-paso

Eric Worral, "A Green Tries to Defend Eco-Terrorism." *WUWT,* November 25, 2017. https://wattsupwiththat.com/2017/11/25/a-green-tries-to-defend-eco-terrorism/

OPPOSING
VIEWPOINTS®
SERIES

CHAPTER 3

Are Politicians and the Media Stoking Domestic Terrorism?

Chapter Preface

Each time there is a new atrocity, a mass shooting, a bombing, or a terrorist attack, the media does its job and reports on the event. The news usually trickles out slowly, particularly the information inquiring minds really want to hear—the killer's name, ethnicity, and motive. People are curious, after all. Because most people would never contemplate perpetrating a mass killing, they are often simultaneously horrified and fascinated by what makes evil people do the things they do.

The media indulges the public's fascination. The names of the murderers are splashed across the front pages of newspapers and the A block of television news shows. These murderers become instantly famous—or notorious. Many of them crave this fame, even in death. "A lot of these shooters want to be treated like celebrities. They want to be famous," says Adam Lankford, a criminologist at the University of Alabama. When Martin Bryant gunned down 35 people in Australia in that country's worst ever mass murder, he was driven in part by notoriety. In the aftermath of his arrest, he continually wanted to know the death toll and what the media had to say about him. As a result, he was prevented from hearing news reports and was only allowed to listen to music on the radio.

Even if common sense suggests that promoting mass murderers is wrong, the media cannot refrain from feeding the beast. As the saying goes, "If it bleeds, it leads." Notorious cult leader Charles Manson, who incited his followers to commit murder, knew exactly how to play the media: when he carved a swastika into his forehead, the media was all too ready to plaster their pages with pictures.

In another case of domestic terrorism, *Rolling Stone,* originally a music periodical that later morphed into providing news coverage and political commentary, took a lot of flak for publishing a flattering picture of Boston marathon bomber Dzhokhar Tsarnaev on its cover. Though the magazine, anticipating the pushback, ran a disclaimer about the importance of Tsarnaev's story as a worthy one to study, the undeniable of effect of his cover picture was that the domestic terrorist looked like a rock star.

Terrorists can breed more terrorists. In 2019, a woman who admired the Columbine High School Killers and who wrote letters to Charleston church murderer Dylann Roof, was convicted of plotting an attack at a Toledo, Ohio, bar and purchasing bomb-making materials to blow up a pipeline in Georgia. Elizabeth Lacron pleaded guilty to terrorism charges. She was sentenced to fifteen years in prison and lifetime supervision upon her release. And who knows who will write letters to her in prison?

Mass shootings appear to be contagious. A 2015 Arizona State University study found that some shooting incidents sparked clusters of subsequent shootings. "High-profile assailants like Newtown's Adam Lanza … are known to have been inspired by past killers. But the ASU team was the first to quantify the effect, finding that school shootings and mass killings—where four or more people are killed—are contagious for an average of 13 days after they occur."[1]

For example, just nine days after the horrific mosque attacks in Queensland, New Zealand, in March 2019, an arsonist set fire to a mosque in Escondido, California. Police found graffiti referencing the Queensland attack at the scene.

Recognizing the link between media publicity and domestic terrorism, many have called upon the media to stop publicizing mass murderers. "The wall-to-wall [media] coverage teaches men who may not be able to get a job or a girlfriend that, nonetheless, in something under an hour, they can become Genghis Khan," writes *The Washington Post's* Megan McCardle.[2] Adam Lankford believes that "the key is to not give them that treatment."[3]

Whether the media can begin to police itself, and exercise constraint in its coverage, remains to be seen. But it is becoming increasingly obvious that lives depend upon it.

Endnotes

1. Nora Kelley, "Are Mass Shootings Contagious?" *The Atlantic.* Dec. 14, 2015. https://www.theatlantic.com/politics/archive/2015/12/mass-shootings-contagious-sandy-hook-san-bernardino/420396/

2. Megan McCardle, Mass murderers crave publicity. Maybe giving them less would be helpful." The Washington Post. Mar. 15, 2019. https://www.washingtonpost.com/opinions/2019/03/15/mass-murderers-crave-publicity-maybe-giving-them-less-would-be-helpful/

3. Lisa Marie Pane, "Should media avoid naming the gunmen in mass shootings?" APNews.com. March 17, 2019 https://apnews.com/00f5376066b8473fa4e0a063d963e89e

> *"Trump was asked whether he would moderate his language after a white nationalist Coast Guard officer was arrested over a plot to assassinate leading journalists and Democrats. 'I think my language is very nice,' he replied."*

President Trump's Rhetoric Has Inspired Mass Shootings

Mehdi Hasan

In the following viewpoint, Medhi Hassan claims that he predicted that right-wing violence would erupt in the wake of hateful rhetoric spewed by right-wing sources. Hassan blames some of this violence on the President of the United States, who has condemned the violence, but who broadcasts the same type of hate speech promulgated by domestic terrorists such as El Paso killer Patrick Crusius and Maga bomber Cesar Sayoc. Hassan believes that President Trump could alleviate some of the tensions by speaking out forcefully against hate. But the president has not done so. Words matter, Hassan states, and what's more the president's words are dangerous. Mehdi Hasan is a senior columnist at the Intercept. He is the host of the Intercept podcast "Deconstructed," as well as of Al Jazeera English's "UpFront."

"After El Paso, We Can No Longer Ignore Trump's Role in Inspiring Mass Shootings," by Mehdi Hasan, The Intercept, August 4, 2019. Reprinted by permission.

As you read, consider the following questions:

1. What specific incidents does the author believe have been partially instigated by presidential rhetoric?
2. What grievances do killers cite that are comparable to those of President Trump?
3. When it comes to hate speech, what is a "dog whistle"?

On Saturday morning, a gunman at a Walmart in El Paso, Texas, shot and killed at least 20 people before surrendering to the police. By all accounts, Patrick Crusius, the 21-year-old alleged shooter, is a fan of President Donald Trump and his policies. According to the Southern Poverty Law Center, a "Twitter account bearing the suspect's name contains liked tweets that include a 'BuildTheWall' hashtag, a photo using guns to spell out 'Trump,'" and more.

Incredibly, the nation woke up to more grim news on Sunday, with reports that a man suited up in body armor and bearing a rifle with high-capacity magazines had carried out a rampage in Dayton, Ohio, killing at least nine people and injuring 26.

Little is known yet about the Dayton shooter, but a four-page manifesto authorities believe was written by Crusius and posted shortly before the El Paso attack is full of the kind of hateful rhetoric and ideas that have flourished under Trump.

The manifesto declares the imminent attack "a response to the Hispanic invasion," accuses Democrats of "pandering to the Hispanic voting bloc," rails against "traitors," and condemns "race mixing" and "interracial unions." "Yet another reason to send them back," it says.

Sound familiar? The president of the United States—who condemned the El Paso attack on Twitter—has repeatedly referred to an "invasion" at the southern border; condemned Mexican immigrants as "rapists" and Syrian refugees as "snakes"; accused his critics of treason on at least two dozen occasions; and told four elected women of color to "go back" to the "crime infested places from which they came." (It is worth noting that Crusius, in his alleged manifesto, claims his views "predate" and are unrelated to Trump but then goes on to attack "fake news.")

That there could be a link between the attacker and the president should come as no surprise. But it might. Over the past four years, both mainstream media organizations and leading Democrats have failed to draw a clear line between Trump's racist rhetoric and the steadily multiplying acts of domestic terror across the United States. Some of us tried to sound the alarm—but to no avail.

"Cesar Sayoc was not the first Trump supporter who allegedly tried to kill and maim those on the receiving end of Trump's demonizing rhetoric," I wrote last October, in the concluding lines of my column on the arrest of the so-called #MAGAbomber. "And, sadly, he won't be the last."

How I wish I could have been proven wrong. Yet since the publication of that piece almost a year ago, which listed the names of more than a dozen Trump supporters accused of horrific violence, from the neo-Nazi murderer of Heather Heyer in Charlottesville to the Quebec City mosque shooter, there have been more and more MAGA-inspired attacks. In January, four men were arrested for a plot to attack a small Muslim community in upstate New York—one of them, according to the Daily Beast, "was an avid Trump supporter online, frequently calling for 'Crooked Hillary' Clinton to be arrested and urging his followers to watch out for Democratic voter fraud schemes when they cast their ballots for Trump in 2016."

In March, a far-right gunman murdered 51 Muslims in two mosques in Christchurch, New Zealand—and left behind a document describing Muslim immigrants as "invaders" and Trump as "a symbol of renewed white identity and common purpose."

And now, this latest massacre in El Paso. Let's be clear: In an age of rising domestic terrorism cases—the majority of which are motivated by "white supremacist violence," according to FBI Director Christopher Wray—Trump is nothing less than a threat to our collective security. More and more commentators now refer, for example, to the phenomenon of "stochastic terrorism"—originally defined by an anonymous blogger back in 2011 as "the use of mass communications to incite random actors to carry out violent or terrorist acts that are *statistically predictable but individually unpredictable.*"

Sounds pretty Trumpian, right? As I wrote in October: "The president may not be pulling the trigger or planting the bomb, but he is enabling much of the hatred behind those acts. He is giving aid and comfort to angry white men by offering them clear targets—and then failing to fully denounce their violence."

And as I pointed out on CNN earlier this year, there is a simple way for Trump to distance himself from all this: Give a speech denouncing white nationalism and the violence it has produced. Declare it a threat to national security. Loudly disown those who act in his name. Tone down the incendiary rhetoric on race, immigration, and Islam.

Trump, however, has done the exact opposite. In March, in the wake of the Christchurch massacre, the president said he did not consider white nationalism to be a rising threat, dismissing it as a "small group of people." A month earlier, in February, Trump was asked whether he would moderate his language after a white nationalist Coast Guard officer was arrested over a plot to assassinate leading journalists and Democrats. "I think my language is very nice," he replied.

In recent weeks, the president has again launched nakedly racist and demagogic attacks on a number of black and brown members of Congress, not to mention the black-majority city of Baltimore. When his cultish supporters responded to his attack on Rep. Ilhan Omar, D-Minn., with chants of "send her back," Trump stood and watched and later referred to them as "patriots."

So we're supposed to be surprised or shocked that white nationalist violence is rising on his watch? That hate crimes against almost every minority group have increased since his election to the White House in 2016?

On Tuesday, just days before this latest act of terror in El Paso, the leaders of the Washington National Cathedral issued a scathing, and startlingly prescient, rebuke of Trump:

> Make no mistake about it, words matter. And, Mr. Trump's words are dangerous.
>
> These words are more than a "dog-whistle." When such violent dehumanizing words come from the President of the United States, they are a clarion call, and give cover, to white supremacists who consider people of color a sub-human "infestation" in America. They serve as a call to action from those people to keep America great by ridding it of such infestation. Violent words lead to violent actions.

Thanks to his hate-filled rhetoric, his relentless incitement of violence, and his refusal to acknowledge the surge in white nationalist terrorism, the president poses a clear and present danger to the people, and especially the minorities, of the United States.

> *"How could the Times possibly
> reconcile that Trump, who
> admonished that the supremacists
> should be 'condemned totally'
> somehow also delivered an
> 'unequivocal boost' to those very
> same miscreants?"*

The Media Has Distorted President Trump's Words

Steve Cortes

In the following viewpoint Steve Cortes argues that the media is promoting a deliberate falsehood to make President Trump look bad. He quotes the president's own words following the tragedy at a white nationalist rally in Charlottesville to argue that Trump never said that neo-Nazis and white nationalists were "fine people." The author asserts the media has stoked criticism of Trump by claiming that he supports white nationalists and that his words gave succor to this group. Instead of hyper-partisan journalism, Cortes writes, we should demand truth from reporters and columnists covering the President. Steve Cortes served as a primary TV surrogate for the Trump presidential campaign and was named to Trump's Hispanic Advisory Council. He is a political commentator for CNN and heads Rise Strategies, a media messaging and public affairs company.

"Trump Didn't Call Neo-Nazis 'Fine People.' Here's Proof," by Steve Cortes, RealClearHoldings, LLC., March 21, 2019. Reprinted by permission.

As you read, consider the following questions:

1. What were President Trump's actual words concerning the Charlottesville march?
2. Did Trump, as some reporters claim, give a boost to white supremacists?
3. How can covering the president as a journalist be difficult, according to the author?

News anchors and pundits have repeated lies about Donald Trump and race so often that some of these narratives seem true, even to Americans who embrace the fruits of the president's policies. The most pernicious and pervasive of these lies is the "Charlottesville Hoax," the fake-news fabrication that he described the neo-Nazis who rallied in Charlottesville, Va., in August 2017 as "fine people."

Just last week I exposed this falsehood, yet again, when CNN contributor Keith Boykin falsely stated, "When violent people were marching with tiki torches in Charlottesville, the president said they were 'very fine people.'" When I objected and detailed that Trump's "fine people on both sides" observation clearly related to those on both sides of the Confederate monument debate, and specifically excluded the violent supremacists, anchor Erin Burnett interjected, "He [Trump] didn't say it was on the monument debate at all. No, they didn't even try to use that defense. It's a good one, but no one's even tried to use it, so you just used it now."

My colleagues seem prepared to dispute our own network's correct contemporaneous reporting and the very clear transcripts of the now-infamous Trump Tower presser on the tragic events of Charlottesville. Here are the unambiguous actual words of President Trump:

> Excuse me, they didn't put themselves down as neo-Nazis, and you had some very bad people in that group. But you also had people that were very fine people on both sides. You had people in that group—excuse me, excuse me, I saw the same pictures

THE USE OF RADICAL ONLINE FORUMS TO SPEW HATE

Thousands of Britons regularly use online forums that espouse rightwing extremism, it has emerged amid fresh warnings that the UK is facing a "new wave" of anti-Muslim hatred.

An indicator of the evolving challenge is the recent move by MI5 to wrest control from the police of investigations into far-right plots that "cross the statutory threshold to be considered terrorism". The security services are currently investigating potential contact between the Christchurch gunman and rightwing extremists in the UK.

Analysis by anti-fascist charity Hope not Hate indicates that huge numbers of Britons are among the global audience for far-right forums—such as Stormfront, the white supremacist website—that spread extremist ideolology.

Sara Khan, the UK's lead anti-extremism commissioner, has pointed to a fresh surge of UK-based far-right activists who are, she says, "organised, professional and actively attempting to recruit".

Khan, who has visited 14 UK towns and cities as she prepares a report on extremism for the home secretary, told the Observer: "I have heard deep concern about the far right and its devastating impact on individuals, communities and our democracy." A "frightening

you did. You had people in that group that were there to protest the taking down of, to them, a very, very important statue and the renaming of a park from Robert E. Lee to another name.

After another question at that press conference, Trump became even more explicit:

I'm not talking about the neo-Nazis and white nationalists because they should be condemned totally.

As a man charged with publicly explaining Donald Trump's often meandering and colloquial vernacular in highly adversarial TV settings, I appreciate more than most the sometimes-murky nature of his off-script commentaries. But these Charlottesville statements leave little room for interpretation. For any honest amount of legal extremist content online" was fuelling far-right activism, she added.

The security services, having placed the threat from rightwing extremist ideology on a par with Islamist and Northern Ireland-related terrorism, have said they are investigating "very sharp high-end cases" in relation to the far right.

So far, though, they have not revealed how many of the 700 or so live terror plots and 20,000 individuals classified as "closed subjects of concern"—people who have previously been investigated and may pose a future threat—are related to rightwing extremism.

However, MI5 said the volume of rightwing cases was "absolutely dwarfed by the number of Islamist cases".

The government's latest counter-terrorism assessment does, however, shed interesting light on the evolving far-right threat. Before 2014, it says, extreme rightwing activity in the UK was confined to "small, established groups with an older membership, which promoted anti-immigration and white supremacist views, but presented a very low risk to national security."

Four extreme rightwing terror plots were foiled in the year to June 2018, fuelling disquiet over online forums and their ability to disseminate extremist ideology.

"Rise in UK Use of Far-Right Online Forums as Anti-Muslim Hate Increases," by Mark Townsend, Guardian News and Media Limited, March 16, 2019.

person, therefore, to conclude that the president somehow praised the very people he actually derided, reveals a blatant and blinding level of bias.

Nonetheless, countless so-called journalists have furthered this damnable lie. For example, MSNBC's Nicolle Wallace responded that Trump had "given safe harbor to Nazis, to white supremacists." Her NBC colleague Chuck Todd claimed Trump "gave me the wrong kind of chills. Honestly, I'm a bit shaken from what I just heard." Not to be outdone, print also got in on the act, with the New York Times spewing the blatantly propagandist headline: "Trump Gives White Supremacists Unequivocal Boost." How could the *Times* possibly reconcile that Trump, who admonished that the supremacists should be "condemned totally" somehow also delivered an "unequivocal boost" to those very same miscreants?

But like many fake news narratives, repetition has helped cement this one into a reasonably plausible storyline for all but the most skeptical consumers of news. In fact, over the weekend, Fox News host Chris Wallace pressed White House Chief of Staff Mick Mulvaney on why Trump has not given a speech "condemning … white supremacist bigotry." Well, Chris, he has, and more than once. The most powerful version was from the White House following Charlottesville and the heartbreaking death of Heather Heyer. President Trump's succinct and direct words:

> Racism is evil, and those who cause violence in its name are criminals and thugs, including the KKK, neo-Nazis, white supremacists, and other hate groups that are repugnant to everything we hold dear as Americans.

Despite the clear evidence of Trump's statements regarding Charlottesville, major media figures insist on spreading the calumny that Trump called neo-Nazis "fine people." The only explanation for such a repeated falsehood is abject laziness or willful deception. Either way, the duplicity on this topic perhaps encapsulates the depressingly low trust most Americans place in major media, with 77 percent stating in a Monmouth University 2018 poll that traditional TV and newspapers report fake news. In addition, such lies as the Charlottesville Hoax needlessly further divide our already-polarized society.

Instead of hyper-partisan, distorted narratives, as American citizens we should demand adherence to truth—and adherence to the common values that bind us regardless of politics. In the words of our president: "No matter the color of our skin, we all live under the same laws, we all salute the same great flag, and we are all made by the same almighty God."

> *"Words matter. Indeed, those two words might be a suitable summary of over a decade of research on the relationship between language and terrorism, which has shown that powerful and emotional narratives are productive."*

Trump's Hate-Filled Words Matter

Jack Holland

In the following viewpoint, Jack Holland argues that President Trump is the world's most prominent "hate-preacher." Trump attacks his political enemies continually, and his words are important because of his office. They give rise to violent acts because through his words the president makes it clear that he condones violence. Words matter, and Trump's words matter more than most. His words are dangerous, the author contends, and Americans must take steps to rectify this situation. Jack Holland is associate professor of international security at the University of Leeds in England. His primary areas of research are US, UK, and Australian foreign and security policy.

"Donald Trump: Words Matter and His Hate Preaching Helps Sponsor Violence," by Jack Holland, The Conversation, November 5, 2018. https://theconversation.com/donald-trump-words-matter-and-his-hate-preaching-helps-sponsor-violence-106026. Licensed under CC BY-ND 4.0 International.

As you read, consider the following questions:

1. What are some specific words President Trump has used that promote a violent response, according to the viewpoint?
2. How has the work of the Founding Fathers been inadequate to deal with a president such as Trump?
3. What avenues to opponents of Trump have to deal with his perceived unfitness for office?

The spate of pipe bombs sent through the mail in the US to prominent liberals was, in many ways, predictable. And the logical upshot of this is that those who have made it so should also bear some responsibility. Yes, someone made the weapons and sent them out—and they must face justice. But we must also acknowledge the role of those who forged the hate-fuelled, increasingly divisive environment in which the attacks took place.

In 2001, George W Bush told the world that the US could no longer afford to make any distinction between terrorists and those who harboured them. Despite the fact that it was hard to find agreement on what "harbour" meant, the role of those sharing and spreading toxic violent ideology was certainly and unanimously included.

Today, President Donald Trump is arguably the world's most prominent hate preacher, inspiring and promoting acts of violence against perceived political enemies. Trump has long revelled in and benefited from the performance of a violent masculinity, hulking over Hillary Clinton, boasting of sexual violence against women, and winning the support of many disaffected and disillusioned American men. Indeed, the day before the pipe bombs began being sent across America, Trump seemingly endorsed the use of violence against political enemies.

"I had heard he body-slammed a reporter," Trump said of Republican Greg Gianforte, who was sentenced to community service and anger management classes after attacking a Guardian journalist. "Anybody that can do a body-slam … that's my kind of guy."

This all builds upon longstanding themes in his personal and national storytelling. The reason the "ordinary American"—the country's backbone—has been so badly downtrodden over the years, he tells voters, is because of continued betrayals and bad deals. America can be made great again—only by him—if the "enemies of the people" are called out and dealt with.

Elites in the media (one of the pipe bombs was also destined for CNN) and the Washington swamp must be drained out of political existence, if America—and true Americans—are to flourish again. And the tactics for doing so, the president of the United States has suggested, can include violence.

Checks and Balances

Words matter. Indeed, those two words might be a suitable summary of over a decade of research on the relationship between language and terrorism, which has shown that powerful and emotional narratives are productive; they create the reality of life in the US, including the wars it fights. Today, that war is at home, between competing wings of the political spectrum. It has turned violent partly because of the language that has been used by the man elected to the highest office in the land.

> Donald J. Trump
> @realDonaldTrump
> There is great anger in our Country caused in part by inaccurate, and even fraudulent, reporting of the news. The Fake News Media, the true Enemy of the People, must stop the open & obvious hostility & report the news accurately & fairly. That will do much to put out the flame...
> 9:18 AM - Oct 29, 2018

When Trump was elected, even among calls not to normalise his ascendancy, many hoped that the Founding Fathers had seen him coming, constructing a system of checks and balances, with adequately divided powers, such that ambition might counteract ambition. To an extent, that was true at the start. But we now see a Supreme Court, both houses of congress, and a White House aligned with a man who apparently encourages violence within the US against American citizens.

Even those who spoke of the need to think of the American government as a hybrid regime—combining democratic and autocratic traits—following Trump's election, might be surprised by how low the country has descended. Fortunately, November—and the mid-term elections—offer an opportunity to begin to change American politics through, rather than by undermining, its democratic credentials.

> *"Fear-based news stories prey on the anxieties we all have and then hold us hostage. Being glued to the television, reading the paper, or surfing the Internet increases ratings and market shares—but it also raises the probability of depression relapse."*

The Media Stokes Fear for Profit

Deborah Serani

In the following viewpoint Deborah Serani asserts that media companies exist for profit and not to provide one-hundred-percent factual accounts of the news. They can generate ratings by using fear as a strong motivator for the viewer to tune in and stay tuned. The success of fear-based news has led companies to replace scientific evidence with arousing stories, she writes. Viewers need to recognize what media companies are doing and take steps to counteract the effects of harmful and duplicitous media. Deborah Serani is a licensed psychologist in practice thirty years. She is also senior adjunct professor at Adelphi University and a TEDx speaker.

"If It Bleeds, It Leads: Understanding Fear-Based Media," by Deborah Serani Psy.D, Sussex Publishers, LLC, June 7, 2011. Reprinted by permission.

As you read, consider the following questions:

1. What are some of the practices media companies follow to generate viewership, according to the viewpoint?
2. How does the use of the crawl generate anxiety and depression?
3. What solutions does the author offer to the viewer?

News is a money-making industry. One that doesn't always make the goal to report the facts accurately. Gone are the days of tuning in to be informed straightforwardly about local and national issues. In truth, watching the news can be a psychologically risky pursuit, which could undermine your mental and physical health.

Fear-based news stories prey on the anxieties we all have and then hold us hostage. Being glued to the television, reading the paper, or surfing the Internet increases ratings and market shares— but it also raises the probability of depression relapse.

In previous decades, the journalistic mission was to report the news as it actually happened, with fairness, balance, and integrity. However, capitalistic motives associated with journalism have forced much of today's television news to look to the spectacular, the stirring, and the controversial as news stories. It's no longer a race to break the story first or get the facts right. Instead, it's to acquire good ratings in order to get advertisers, so that profits soar.

News programming uses a hierarchy of if it bleeds, it leads. Fear-based news programming has two aims. The first is to grab the viewer's attention. In the news media, this is called the teaser. The second aim is to persuade the viewer that the solution for reducing the identified fear will be in the news story. If a teaser asks, "What's in your tap water that YOU need to know about?" a viewer will likely tune in to get the up-to-date information to ensure safety.

The success of fear-based news relies on presenting dramatic anecdotes in place of scientific evidence, promoting isolated events as trends, depicting categories of people as dangerous and replacing optimism with fatalistic thinking. News conglomerates who want to achieve this use media logic, by tweaking the rhythm, grammar, and presentation format of news stories to elicit the greatest impact. Did you know that some news stations work with consultants who offer fear-based topics that are pre-scripted, outlined with point-of-view shots, and have experts at-the-ready? This practice is known as stunting or just-add-water reporting. Often, these practices present misleading information and promote anxiety in the viewer.

Another pattern in newscasts is that the breaking news story doesn't go beyond a surface level. The need to get-the-story-to-get-the-ratings often causes reporters to bypass thorough fact-checking. As the first story develops to a second level in later reports, the reporter corrects the inaccuracies and missing elements. As the process of fact-finding continually changes, so does the news story. What journalists first reported with intense emotion or sensationalism is no longer accurate. What occurs psychologically for the viewer is a fragmented sense of knowing what's real, which sets off feelings of hopelessness and helplessness—experiences known to worsen depression.

An additional practice that heightens anxiety and depression is the news station's use of the crawl, the scrolling headline ticker that appears at the bottom of the television, communicating "breaking news." Individuals who watch news-based programming are likely to see one, two, or even three crawls scroll across the screen. The multitasking required to read the crawls and comprehend the actual newscast comes easy to some viewers, whereas others report feeling over-stimulated.

One could easily change the channel to interrupt the transmission of such information. However, crawls are not relegated to just news channels. Unlike the viewing experience of the past, crawls are now more prominent during entertainment programs and often serve as commercials for nightly newscasts or the upcoming weekly news magazine show. The crawls frequently contain fear-driven material, broad-siding an unsuspecting viewer.

It's been said that fear-based media has become a staple of popular culture. The distressing fall-out from this trend is that children and adults who are exposed to media are more likely than others to

- Feel that their neighborhoods and communities are unsafe
- Believe that crime rates are rising
- Overestimate their odds of becoming a victim
- Consider the world to be a dangerous place

News media needs to return to a sense of proportion, conscience, and, most important, *truth-telling*. Until that happens, help inoculate yourself against feeling overwhelmed by doing the following:

- Consider limiting your exposure to media. Give yourself a set time once or twice a day to check in on local and global happenings.
- Consider choosing print media for your information gathering rather than visual media. This can reduce the likelihood that you get exposed to emotionally laden material. Home pages on the internet can give you an overall sense of what's going on, as can headline news channels that update stories on the hour.
- Remember that you have the power to turn off the remote, leave a website, or change the radio station. Don't let yourself be passive when you feel media is overwhelming you.
- Know that other people will have a different tolerance for media stories and their details. If someone is expressing too much of a story for your own comfort, walk away or communicate your distress.
- Consider having an electronic-free day, and let your senses take in the simpler things in life.

References

Altheide, D. (2002). Creating fear: News and the construction of crisis. New York: Walter de Gruyter.

Gerbner, G., Morgan, M., & Signorielli, N. (1999). Profiling television violence. In K. Nordenstreng & M. Griffin (Eds.), International media monitoring (pp. 335-365). Hillsdale, NJ: Hampton Press.

Glassner, B. (1999). The culture of fear: Why Americans are afraid of the wrong things. New York: Basic Books.

Kovach, B., & Rosenthal, T. (2001). The elements of journalism: What news-people should know and the public should expect. New York: Three Rivers Press.

Serani, D. (2008). If it bleeds, it leads. The clinical implications of fear-based programming in news media. Psychotherapy and Psychoanalysis, 24(4), 240-250.

> "*The growth of online activities by white nationalist groups in the United States and beyond—a phenomenon highlighted again by the El Paso incident—indicates that countries and social media platforms have been slow to confront this threat.*"

Social Media Has Facilitated Domestic Terrorism

David P. Fidler

In the following viewpoint David P. Fidler discusses the correlation between social media and domestic terrorism. Social media has made it easier for fringe elements to spread propaganda and hate speech. Insufficient strides have been made toward curtailing such incendiary speech online. The 2019 mass shooting in an El Paso Walmart highlights how difficult it has been to limit unacceptable online behavior. But when fighting extremist online speech, authorities must also confront the behavior of authority figures and politicians who have used fear and resentment to gain power. David P. Fidler is adjunct senior fellow for cybersecurity and global health at the Council on Foreign Relations and visiting professor at the Washington University School of Law in St. Louis.

As you read, consider the following questions:

1. How has the El Paso shooting brought attention to online forums such as 8chan?
2. What recommendations for fighting online hate speech have been made by the International Cyber Terrorism Regulation Project (ICTRP)?
3. Why is fighting online behavior that incites domestic terrorism even more difficult than fighting behavior that stokes Islamic terrorism, according to the author?

Here we go again. The violence in El Paso, Texas has re-fueled debates about domestic terrorism, gun control, whether President Donald J. Trump's rhetoric contributes to violent extremism, and the role cyberspace plays in fostering extremist hatred and violence. The Department of Justice is treating the El Paso incident as domestic terrorism, and the manifesto the suspect posted online before the attack contributed to this decision. The manifesto appeared on a social media site, 8chan, already notorious as a platform used by perpetrators and supporters of mass violence. Indeed, prior to the El Paso tragedy, 8chan was, as the *New York Times* put it, "a megaphone for mass shooters, and a recruiting platform for violent white nationalists."

The post-El Paso replaying of debates about white nationalism as terrorism and about extremist groups' use of social media suggests that insufficient progress has been made in curbing white nationalism's growth and cyberspace's contribution to that expansion. This incident underscores the need to take stock, again, of strategies for addressing how terrorist and extremist groups exploit the internet to spread hate and incite violence.

A few days before the El Paso attack, the International Cyber Terrorism Regulation Project (ICTRP) released findings and recommendations. The ICTRP is supported by the Global Research Network on Terrorism and Technology coordinated by the Royal United Services Institute and is led by the International

Institute for Counter-Terrorism. The project is analyzing how governments, international organizations, and private-sector enterprises combat the online activities of terrorist groups. By cataloging components of the "regulatory toolbox," the project seeks to make policy and legal strategies more transparent, identify how and why strategies around the world are similar and different, and generate recommendations for improving public and private actions to mitigate terrorist use of the internet. (Along with other experts, I provided input to this project.)

The ICTRP's analytical framework maps strategies adopted by governments, international organizations, and companies against the ways that terrorists exploit the internet. From this exercise, the ICTRP developed findings that are relevant to post-El Paso debates. First, the project found that common definitions of prohibited terrorist internet activities are lacking within and across jurisdictional lines. Second, most national jurisdictions do not have "an overarching conceptual and strategic approach to counterterrorism on the internet." Third, policies developed by social media companies to address terrorism online frequently differ between jurisdictions.

The growth of online activities by white nationalist groups in the United States and beyond—a phenomenon highlighted again by the El Paso incident—indicates that countries and social media platforms have been slow to confront this threat. Unlike the social media exploits of the so-called Islamic State, governments and companies have struggled more to associate white nationalism with terrorism, including with respect to cyber activities. This situation arises from various factors, including the difficulty of defining terrorism and identifying what terrorist online activities governments and the private-sector should prohibit in light of the potent re-emergence of nationalism, xenophobia, and racial and ethnic prejudice as political forces in many countries.

The designation of the El Paso violence as domestic terrorism underscores the second ICTRP finding—the continued lack of overarching national strategies for counterterrorism on the internet designed to prevent extremist violence. Despite warnings that pre-date the Trump administration about the dangers that online white nationalist efforts pose, US political discourse on white nationalism as a form of violent extremism spreading via the internet has generated more sound and fury than strategic coherence in counterterrorism policy.

The El Paso tragedy also re-focused scrutiny on 8chan as an outlet for the hatred and violence associated with white nationalism. News reports discussed differences in how social media platforms have responded to online activities of white nationalists, with 8chan doing nothing and other platforms, such as Facebook and Twitter, making attempts to keep this form of extremism off its services. The posting of another white nationalism screed on 8chan by a mass killer also prompted tech companies that provide services to 8chan to struggle with how to respond to extremist violence intertwined with internet behavior, with Cloudfare deciding to terminate 8chan as a customer. What happened before and after the El Paso killings provides another case study in the variations in social media companies' policies for addressing online terrorism.

The ICTRP report also included recommendations for improving public and private strategies vis-à-vis terrorist activities online, including the need for:

- More strategic, multidimensional, and multi-stakeholder cooperation;
- Providing small and mid-sized social media platforms with capacity-building resources;
- Increased information sharing about public and private regulatory measures; and
- More use of technological tools (e.g., artificial intelligence).

The El Paso episode highlights how difficult these recommendations might be to implement. If the transnational proliferation of white nationalist activities in cyberspace and their connection with multiple episodes of extremist violence have not provoked more strategic cooperation, what crisis will do so?

The role of 8chan and other cyber sanctuaries that nurture white nationalist ideologies does not arise from incapacities in these social media platforms, a lack of information about policies and laws, or insufficient use of machine learning.

Further research can refine the ICTRP's findings and recommendations in light of how different forms of terrorism manifest themselves online, affect domestic politics, and shape public and private policymaking and lawmaking processes. Even so, confronting white nationalism's exploitation of the internet will prove more contentious than anything experienced in counterterrorism policy's targeting of Islamic extremism's online endeavors. Such a confrontation will not be able to avoid how political leaders in a number of countries, including the United States, have stoked racial and xenophobic fear and resentment in order to gain influence and exercise power.

> *"As far back as 2011, the US Supreme Court ruled that research did not find a clear connection between violent video games and aggressive behavior."*

Stop Blaming Video Games for Mass Killings

Christopher Ferguson

In the following viewpoint Christopher Ferguson, a researcher who has studied violent video games for almost fifteen years, asserts that there is no evidence to support claims that video games and real-world violence are connected. Those who conduct research in this area consider the linkage a myth. Yet politicians continue to maintain that violent video games are linked to domestic terrorism and mass murder. According to Ferguson, spikes in video game usage tend to correlate with decreases in youth violence. Groups such as the National Rifle Association and American Psychological Association, each of whom has an agenda, have spread false information about video games and violence. In doing so, they each make it more difficult to address real issues such as mental health and gun control. Christopher Ferguson is a professor of psychology at Stetson University in Florida. He is coauthor of Moral Combat: Why the War on Violent Video Games is Wrong.

As you read, consider the following questions:

1. Why do many policymakers blame violent video games for violence, according to the viewpoint?
2. How does the author support his claim that spikes in video game play are associated with drops in youth violence?
3. Why do groups such as the National Rifle Association and American Psychological Association spread false information about video games and societal violence?

In the wake of the El Paso shooting on Aug. 3 that left 22 dead and dozens injured, a familiar trope has reemerged: Often, when a young man is the shooter, people try to blame the tragedy on violent video games and other forms of media.

This time around, Texas Lt. Gov. Dan Patrick placed some of the blame on a video game industry that "teaches young people to kill." Republican House Minority Leader Kevin McCarthy of California went on to condemn video games that "dehumanize individuals" as a "problem for future generations." And President Trump pointed to society's "glorification of violence," including "gruesome and grisly video games."

These are the same connections a Florida lawmaker made after the Parkland shooting in February 2018, suggesting that the gunman in that case "was prepared to pick off students like it's a video game."

But, as a researcher who has studied violent video games for almost 15 years, I can state that there is no evidence to support these claims that violent media and real-world violence are connected.

As far back as 2011, the US Supreme Court ruled that research did not find a clear connection between violent video games and aggressive behavior. Criminologists who study mass shootings specifically refer to those sorts of connections as a "myth." And in 2017, the Media Psychology and Technology division of the American Psychological Association released a statement I helped craft, suggesting reporters and policymakers cease linking mass shootings to violent media, given the lack of evidence for a link.

A History of a Moral Panic

So why are so many policymakers inclined to blame violent video games for violence? There are two main reasons.

The first is the psychological research community's efforts to market itself as strictly scientific. This led to a replication crisis instead, with researchers often unable to repeat the results of their studies. Now, psychology researchers are reassessing their analyses of a wide range of issues—not just violent video games, but implicit racism, power poses and more.

The other part of the answer lies in the troubled history of violent video game research specifically.

Beginning in the early 2000s, some scholars, anti-media advocates and professional groups like the APA began working to connect a methodologically messy and often contradictory set of results to public health concerns about violence. This echoed historical patterns of moral panic, such as 1950s concerns about comic books and Tipper Gore's efforts to blame pop and rock music in the 1980s for violence, sex and Satanism.

Particularly in the early 2000s, dubious evidence regarding violent video games was uncritically promoted. But over the years, confidence among scholars that violent video games influence aggression or violence has crumbled.

Reviewing All the Scholarly Literature

My own research has examined the degree to which violent video games can—or can't—predict youth aggression and violence. In a 2015 meta-analysis, I examined 101 studies on the subject and found that violent video games had little impact on kids' aggression, mood, helping behavior or grades.

Two years later, I found evidence that scholarly journals' editorial biases had distorted the scientific record on violent video games. Experimental studies that found effects were more likely to

RESEARCH FINDS NO CONNECTION BETWEEN VIOLENT VIDEO GAMES AND MASS SHOOTINGS

Two deadly mass shootings occurred within 24 hours of one another this weekend—one in El Paso, Texas and the other in Dayton, Ohio. Thirty-one people have died from their injuries so far.

Some Republicans, including President Donald Trump, have argued that violent video games are partially to blame for the violence.

"We must stop the glorification of violence in our society. This includes the gruesome and grisly video games that are now commonplace," Trump said Monday during public remarks addressing the violence in El Paso and Dayton.

Whitney DeCamp is a professor of sociology at Western Michigan University. He researches the connection between violence and video games. DeCamp says his research has found that playing violent video games does not contribute to real-life violence.

Instead, DeCamp says, it comes from seeing violence within the home and community.

be published than studies that had found none. This was consistent with others' findings. As the Supreme Court noted, any impacts due to video games are nearly impossible to distinguish from the effects of other media, like cartoons and movies.

Any claims that there is consistent evidence that violent video games encourage aggression are simply false.

Spikes in violent video games' popularity are well-known to correlate with substantial declines in youth violence—not increases. These correlations are very strong, stronger than most seen in behavioral research. More recent research suggests that the releases of highly popular violent video games are associated with immediate declines in violent crime, hinting that the releases may cause the drop-off.

> "I think those comments ignore the fact that we already have a lot of evidence on this topic. And that evidence is pointing to a pretty solid 'no' on video games being the cause of real life violence," he said.
>
> DeCamp says that politicians who blame video games are looking for a scapegoat. In the case of El Paso, the suspected shooter released a racist and anti-immigrant manifesto prior to inflicting mass carnage.
>
> "We can see specifically that it's hateful rhetoric that's directed at immigrants and racial and ethnic minorities that's been a large motivating factor there," Decamp said. "But it's a convenient way to change the discussion away from other issues that might be more controversial and harder to deal with, like the issue of gun availability, mental health, and hateful rhetoric that is out there."
>
> It's easier, DeCamp says, to blame video games for gun violence because it doesn't require any immediate change. Video games are protected under the First Amendment, which means regulating their content would require an amendment to the Constitution.
>
> **"Research Contradicts Claim That Violent Video Games Share Blame for Mass Shootings," by Stateside Staff, Michigan Radio, August 5, 2019.**

The Role of Professional Groups

With so little evidence, why are lawmakers still trying to blame violent video games for mass shootings by young men? Can groups like the National Rifle Association seriously blame imaginary guns for gun violence?

A key element of that problem is the willingness of professional guild organizations such as the APA to promote false beliefs about violent video games. (I'm a fellow of the APA.) These groups mainly exist to promote a profession among news media, the public and policymakers, influencing licensing and insurance laws. They also make it easier to get grants and newspaper headlines. Psychologists and psychology researchers like myself pay them yearly dues to increase the public profile of psychology. But there is a risk the general public may mistake promotional positions for objective science.

In 2005 the APA released its first policy statement linking violent video games to aggression. However, my recent analysis of internal APA documents with criminologist Allen Copenhaver found that the APA ignored inconsistencies and methodological problems in the research data.

The APA updated its statement in 2015, but that sparked controversy immediately: More than 230 scholars wrote to the group asking it to stop releasing policy statements altogether. I and others objected to perceived conflicts of interest and lack of transparency tainting the process.

It's bad enough that these statements misrepresent the actual scholarly research and misinform the public. But it's worse when those falsehoods give advocacy groups like the NRA cover to shift blame for violence onto non-issues like video games. The resulting misunderstanding hinders efforts to address mental illness and other issues, such as the need for gun control, that are actually related to gun violence.

Periodical and Internet Sources Bibliography

The following articles have been selected to supplement the diverse views presented in this chapter.

David Atkins, "Trump Still Refuses to Condemn Violent White Supremacy." *Washington Monthly*, August 4, 2019. https://washingtonmonthly.com/2019/08/04/trump-still-refuses-to-condemn-violent-white-supremacy/

Ken Brenner, "How the Media Fuels Terrorism…and What Can Be Done." *Radio + Television Business Report*, August 16, 2019. https://www.rbr.com/media-terrorism-benner/

Matt Dessem, "Fox News Had to Interrupt Its Border Scaremongering to Report the El Paso Shooting." Slate, August 4, 2019. https://slate.com/news-and-politics/2019/08/el-paso-shooting-fox-breaking-news-garrett-tenney-gillian-turner.html

David P. Fidler, "Terrorism, Social Media, and the El Paso Tragedy." Council on Foreign Relations, August 6, 2019. https://www.cfr.org/blog/terrorism-social-media-and-el-paso-tragedy

Jim Geraghty, "No, Fox News Does Not Inspire Terrorism." *National Review*, July 23, 2019. https://www.nationalreview.com/corner/no-fox-news-does-not-inspire-terrorism/

Ben Gilbert, "One glaring piece of evidence refutes the claim that playing violent video games causes gun violence." Business Insider, March 4, 2018. https://www.businessinsider.com/video-games-gun-violence-2018-3

April Glaser, "Why Social Media Surveillance Alone Won't Prevent Hate-Fueled Mass Shootings." Slate, August 28, 2019. https://slate.com/technology/2019/08/el-paso-walmart-social-media-violence-threats-arrests.html

W.J. Henningan, "How Big a Role Does Social Media Play in Homegrown Terrorism?" *Time*, October 30, 2018. https://time.com/5438481/terrorism-social-media/

Erin M. Kearns and Amarnath Amarasingam, "How News Media Talk About Terrorism: What the Evidence Shows." Just Security, April 5, 2019. https://www.justsecurity.org/63499/how-news-media-talk-about-terrorism-what-the-evidence-shows/

Jared Keller, "The DOJ Is Finally Bridging the Gap Between Online Radicalization and Domestic Terrorism." *Pacific Standard*, August 5, 2019. https://psmag.com/social-justice/the-doj-is-finally-bridging-the-gap-between-online-radicalization-and-domestic-terrorism

David Sherfinski, "Texas Lt. Gov. Dan Patrick laments video games, social media after El Paso shooting." *Washington Times,* August 4, 2017. https://www.nationalreview.com/2017/06/masculinity-not-toxic-stop-blaming-men-everything/

C. J. Werleman, "The El Paso Killer Loved Trump. Do You? Then You're Responsible, Too." *Forward*, August 3, 2019. https://forward.com/opinion/428847/the-el-paso-shooter-supported-trump-if-you-do-too-you-are-supporting-the/

Lara White, "Has Trump's White House 'resurrected' Army of God anti-abortion extremists?" Open Democracy, Feb. 5, 2018. https://www.opendemocracy.net/en/5050/army-of-god-anti-abortion-terrorists-emboldened-under-trump/

Christina Zhao, "Trump Administration Is 'Facilitating and Enabling' Youth to Commit 'Terrorism,' Ex-FBI Official Says After El Paso Shooting." *Newsweek*, August 3, 2019. https://www.newsweek.com/trump-administration-facilitating-enabling-youth-commit-terrorism-ex-fbi-official-says-1452473

CHAPTER 4

How Can Domestic Terrorism Be Prevented?

Chapter Preface

Undoubtedly, domestic terrorism will continue in some fashion even if every one of the typical proposed solutions is enacted: exercising gun control; banning violent video games, films, and television shows; improving mental health. There is no panacea. But the United States is particularly vulnerable to attack precisely because of the many freedoms Americans enjoy. And the most consequential freedom with regard to domestic terrorism is granted by the second amendment: the right to bear arms. The easy accessibility of weaponry in the United States, particularly of semi-automatic rifles such as the AR-15, has come with a price. "The United States has the 28th-highest rate of deaths from gun violence in the world: 4.43 deaths per 100,000 people in 2017—far greater than what is seen in other wealthy countries."[1]

The arguments against gun control have become clichés that everyone has heard: "Guns don't kill people. People kill people." "The only thing that stops a bad guy with a gun is a good guy with a gun." "If guns are banned only criminals will have guns."

And yet, real life belies these clichés. After the worst mass murder in Australian history, Martin Bryant's killing of 36 people in Port Arthur, Tasmania, in 1996, the Australian government took some rather austere measures. Shortly after the tragedy, Australia enacted the National Firearms Agreement. The laws placed tight controls on semi-automatic and automatic weapons, essentially banning them from importation or ownership by the average Australian. A gun buyback program was also instituted, and many Australians—somewhat surprisingly—agreed to give up their weapons.

In its early history, Australia, like the United States, had a rough-and-tumble reputation. As Clifton Leaf writes in *Fortune* magazine it was "A land of roughneck pioneers and outback settlers." Australia was not a country that embraced regulation, and certainly not regulation of firearms. Leaf continues, "This was a land of almost cartoonish toughness and self-reliance, home of Crocodile Dundee and Australian rules football … . But Port Arthur had followed too many prior deadly shooting sprees and Australians were clearly sick to death of them."[2]

The results could have been predicted: mass murders in Australia all but ended. This is not to say that no attacks occurred: Australians were shocked to learn that a gunman killed four people in June 2019 using a banned weapon, a 12-gauge pump action shotgun, that authorities speculated may have been stolen as far back as 1997. But the overall decline in gun violence was dramatic: Australia became a safer place to live.

Unlike Australians, Americans will never give up their guns. That much is clear. Various surveys estimate that Americans own approximately 400 million firearms, and that 30–40 percent of US households have at least one gun. While some states, usually those described as "blue" or left-leaning, tighten gun laws, "red" or more conservative states, have loosened theirs. In many cases, under current laws, there is little authorities can do.

As Stephen N. Xenakis writes for *USA Today*, "The startling fact about the shooter in El Paso, Texas, is that his mother called the police to warn them that he was buying automatic weapons. And what did the police say to her? He is an adult and can legally purchase these guns."[3] One might argue that, at the very least, the authorities could have kept track of Patrick Crusius, who eventually used his weaponry on innocent Walmart shoppers. Perhaps they should have known that he failed a background check to buy weapons due to his mental health issues, then bought his AR-15 in a private transaction that, according to the law, required no background check. But why should they have, when the transaction was technically legal?

Crusius's mental health should have been a red flag for authorities, but in a state where gun laws are lax at best, it wasn't. For this reason many supporters of sensible gun control are advocating for red flag laws, which allow police or family members to petition a state court to order the temporary removal of firearms from a person who may present a danger to others or themselves. Perhaps Crusius's mother could have helped prevent the tragedy if such a law were in effect in Texas.

This scenario is unlikely to occur. Texas is among the most lenient of states when it comes to gun laws. And even with red flag laws it is certain that some would-be domestic terrorists will fall through the cracks. But one thing is certain: without stricter gun laws, there will be many more successful American domestic terrorists in the years to come.

Endnotes

1. Nurith Aizenman and Marc Silver "How The US Compares With Other Countries In Deaths From Gun Violence." *NPR*. August 5, 2019. https://www.npr.org/sections/goatsandsoda/2019/08/05/743579605/how-the-u-s-compares-to-other-countries-in-deaths-from-gun-violence

2. Clifton Leaf, "How Australia All But Ended Gun Violence." Fortune. Febraury 20, 2018. https://fortune.com/2018/02/20/australia-gun-control-success/

3. Stephen N. Xenakis, "After Odessa: We need a military-scale fight against domestic terrorism and gun violence." *USA Today*. Sept. 5, 2019. https://www.usatoday.com/story/opinion/2019/09/05/fight-gun-violence-domestic-terror-like-we-fought-islamic-state-column/2197369001/

| "A smart, comprehensive and sustainable national framework to prevent violent extremist attacks is long overdue."

Prioritizing Development of a Prevention Framework Is Important When Responding to the Rise in Domestic Terrorism

Eric Rosand

In the following viewpoint, Eric Rosand asserts that resources for dealing with domestic terrorism are minuscule when compared with those allotted to radical Islamic terrorism. Therefore, increased attention to domestic terrorism, long overdue, is a necessity. Rosand calls for a "national framework" that includes numerous actors and programs to identify early threats and counteract domestic terrorism. Rosand highlights numerous steps that may be taken to create this framework in an era when domestic terrorist activities are likely to increase. Eric Rosand is a nonresident senior fellow in the Project on US Relations with the Islamic World at Brookings and director of "The Prevention Project: Organizing against Violent Extremism" in Washington, D.C.

As you read, consider the following questions:

1. According to the viewpoint, how has the United States lagged behind other countries facing domestic terrorism in addressing the problem?
2. What steps does the author suggest to create a national framework for attacking the threat of domestic terrorism?
3. Why are incidents of domestic terrorism likely to increase, according to the author?

The April attack on a synagogue in Poway, California, was the latest demonstration of the rise in extremist violence in the United States committed not by "jihadists" inspired by ISIS or other international terrorists, but by white supremacists, neo-Nazis or other right-wing groups. With the Tree of Life Synagogue attacks still fresh in many Americans' minds, post-Poway discussions further highlighted how the resources and tools available to prevent right-wing extremist violence or domestic terrorism in the United States are dwarfed by those available to deal with the jihadist-inspired violence that data shows to be a much lesser threat. Rectifying this imbalance requires urgent attention.

The response to recent right-wing violence has emphasized the need for tougher laws, with some commentators urging Congress to adopt a domestic terrorism statute that includes the "material support" clause that exists for international terrorism. This would allow law enforcement to intervene at early stages of attack planning and plotting. Some experts have argued that a list of domestic terrorist groups should be created, modeled, where appropriate, on the one the Department of State maintains for foreign terrorist organizations. There have also been repeated calls, including by congressional leaders, for the Federal Bureau of Investigation and the Department of Homeland Security (DHS) to increase their data collection and analytic capabilities on this issue and for more intelligence sharing on right-wing threats with other countries. Ensuring federal law-enforcement agencies have the resources and tools needed to prioritize the investigation and prosecution of domestic terrorist has also received attention. House Committee on Homeland Security Chairman Bennie Thompson has led the charge to pressure social media companies to do more to crack down on the use of their platforms by right-wing organizations, that is, taking steps similar to those they have taken against extremist content linked to ISIS and other jihadi groups. There have also been proposals to make more funding available to protect religious institutions and other "soft targets" from terrorist attacks.

The increased attention to right-wing or domestic terrorism is long overdue, and each of the above steps deserves serious consideration. However, by largely limiting the focus to the existing counterterrorism tool kit and how it can be applied to the rising right-wing threat in the United States, we are in danger of adopting the same overly narrow, security-driven approach to preventing domestic terrorism that has characterized efforts against jihadi-inspired violence at home. We need a national framework that includes an ecosystem of actors and programs that extends beyond law enforcement and involves mental health professionals, social workers, teachers, religious and other community leaders, parents, nongovernmental organizations, and the private sector (beyond just social media companies).

Mind the Gap

Virtually every industrialized country that faces extremist violence threats has developed a national framework that outlines the roles and responsibilities of actors at the national and local levels and across law-enforcement and non-law-enforcement disciplines (see, for example, Canada, Denmark, and Switzerland). Such frameworks lay the foundations for multidisciplinary local programs that can intercede with individuals showing observable signs of being at risk of, vulnerable to or already on the path of radicalization to violence—regardless of their ideological, political or other motivation. These mechanisms aim to stop the path to violence at an early stage, enabling the mobilization of professionals and other community members who may be better placed to deliver an effective and preventive intervention because they have particular competence, expertise or perceived credibility or legitimacy that the police do not possess.

These programs are primarily for concerned family or other community members who suspect that an individual is becoming radicalized but has not yet committed to violence. (They also offer the police an option between arrest and doing nothing. This is important when dealing with individuals who have yet to commit a crime but could put people's lives at risk if they don't receive some form of intervention, and it encourages family members who are understandably reluctant to work with authorities if it means their loved ones end up in jail.) Prior studies have shown that for three out of four persons who go on to commit violent attacks, their family or friends knew that something was seriously awry, but they did not get help, call the police or stop the attack. This is often because they do not know whom to call other than the police and are often reluctant to make that call and potentially risk heavy law-enforcement action. Many of these programs rely on psychologists, religious leaders or former extremists to help individuals, whether associated with right-wing or jihadi groups, to disengage from violence.

Many of the ecosystems of programs enacted by US allies are due, at least in part, to the generous and long-term national-level funding and guidance that have been made available to support locally led efforts to develop and sustain extremist violence prevention (and disengagement) initiatives framed around the concerns of specific communities. Yet the United States has become the outlier.

Even before President Trump, US efforts at countering violent extremism (CVE)—which focused primarily on jihadi-related extremism—were championed primarily by government officials but attracted little public or local support. Those on the political left tended to see CVE efforts at home as too law-enforcement oriented and raised concerns about the targeting of American

Muslims and the violation of their civil liberties. Those on the right felt they lacked metrics and were too politically correct—and thus were insufficiently focused on what they (despite the evidence) saw as the "real" threat of "radical Islam." Many communities around the country that might want to become more involved in local initiatives to prevent extremist violence have felt excluded from what they perceived to be an overly securitized, Washington-centric conversation that was perceived (rightly or wrongly) to be about preventing future ISIS and al-Qaeda-inspired attacks, and not about extremist or targeted violence more broadly, including right-wing and gang violence. These stakeholders felt that CVE programs did not sufficiently take into account their broader concerns, which often were linked to rising levels of Islamophobia and broader feelings of discrimination and stigmatization.

As has been well documented, the Trump administration cut federal resources for preventing extremist violence, including not renewing the one-time $10 million local grants program and significantly downsizing the relevant DHS office. More broadly, the Trump administration, despite the rhetoric on "domestic terrorism" in its 2018 counterterrorism strategy, ignored a congressional request to produce a strategy for countering violent extremism both at home and abroad.

The polarizing and politicized debates in the United States around CVE efforts have not allowed the space for a serious, practical discussion about how best to prevent extremist violence at home that is informed by the existing data and evidence. A more serious approach should incorporate good practices and lessons learned from US allies in Europe, as well as Australia and Canada, all of which are confronted by both jihadi and right-wing threats.

Seize the Day

The current spotlight on right-wing extremist violence in the United States—and the widely available data showing that it, and not jihadi-inspired violence, is a much greater threat to cities and communities around the country—creates a unique opportunity to move beyond the unproductive CVE debates of the past few years. It's time for a more productive conversation that includes communities that are concerned about extremist violence of any stripe affecting them and want to contribute to prevention efforts. A smart, comprehensive and sustainable national framework to prevent violent extremist attacks is long overdue. A better approach must go beyond investigations, prosecutions and arrests; involve more than just removing extremist content from social media platforms; and rally the support of the Departments of Health and Human Services and Education, alongside the federal law-enforcement agencies, and state, local and community-level actors and organizations.

Core elements of a framework could include the following:

- An emphasis on government collaboration and engagement with communities.
- The involvement of professionals from across different disciplines, such as mental health, social work, mentoring and education.
- A national network connecting front-line practitioners and professionals working to prevent different forms of extremist violence in their communities.
- An approach based on evidence rather than on assumptions.
- The development of nondiscriminatory tools to enable professionals and community members to better identify those most at risk or vulnerable to committing acts of extremist violence and local programs that can address those risk factors and vulnerabilities.
- A small-grants program, ideally overseen by the Department of Health and Human Services, that provides funding and guidance to community-based and other local organizations interested in starting new or scaling up existing programs aimed at preventing extremist violence, but framed around local concerns.
- More broadly, the adoption of a public health (as opposed to a law-enforcement-driven) approach to preventing extremist

violence, which offers opportunities for multipurpose programming, avoiding stigma, and leveraging existing public health resources, including mental health professionals, social workers or teachers.

Regrettably, given the current rhetoric, tensions and political climate, levels of hate-inspired and other extremist violence in the United States are unlikely to dip in the coming years and may even worsen. As such, the issue of how to address this extremism is unlikely to go away. Rather than simply relying on the existing playbook, political leaders, policymakers and practitioners would be wise to prioritize the development of this missing prevention framework.

| "*The creation of a federal crime of domestic terrorism would also counter the widespread but incorrect notion that the federal government does not care about domestic terrorism.*"

Congress Must Make Domestic Terrorism a Federal Crime

Mary B. McCord

In the following viewpoint Mary B. McCord argues that, given recent events, it is time to enact a federal designation of domestic terrorism. Islamic extremists who commit violent acts are currently identified as terrorists, yet extremists who commit atrocities domestically are not. This does not make sense to McCord, who cites several instances of domestic extremist actions that have not been designated as terrorist incidents. This causes problems with prosecution of domestic terrorists; the solution is to enact a federal crime of domestic terrorism. For McCord, the benefits of doing so outweigh potential problems. Mary B. McCord is legal director and visiting professor of law at the Institute for Constitutional Advocacy and Protection at Georgetown University Law School. She is the former Acting Assistant Attorney General and Principal Deputy Assistant Attorney General for National Security at the US Department of Justice.

"It's Time for Congress to Make Domestic Terrorism a Federal Crime," by Mary B. McCord, visiting professor, Georgetown University Law Center, published by the Lawfare Institute, December 5, 2018. Reprinted by permission.

As you read, consider the following questions:

1. What distinguishes an act of international terrorism from one of domestic terrorism?
2. What issues are raised by the lack of a federal crime of domestic terrorism?
3. What problems might arise from creating a federal designation of domestic terrorism?

On Oct. 27, Robert Bowers launched an attack on the Tree of Life Synagogue in Pittsburgh, Pennsylvania, murdering 11 worshipers and injuring many others. The federal indictment against Bowers charges him with multiple counts of obstructing, by force and threat of force, "the free exercise of religious beliefs" resulting in death and bodily injury and involving the use of a dangerous weapon and attempts to kill. These counts are charged under a suite of federal hate crimes statutes first enacted in 1968 and amended periodically ever since. Some of these crimes allow for the maximum sentence under law: the death penalty. But they fail to hold Robert Bowers accountable for what he actually did: commit crimes of domestic terrorism.

Bowers is just as morally deserving of the "terrorist" label as Islamist extremists who engage in acts of violence to intimidate and coerce. That label carries weight—it creates a moral equivalency between domestic terrorists and international terrorists, and it signals to Americans that the threat of extremism is just as significant when it is based on domestic political, economic, religious or social ideologies as it is when based on Islamist extremist ideologies. This has become ever more important as the United States experiences increased incidents of violence, and threats of violence, perpetrated on behalf of extremist right-wing ideologies. There are no good terrorists, domestic or international. It is time for Congress to enact a federal offense of domestic terrorism.

I recently had occasion to talk about domestic terrorism at a summit in St. Louis as part of Communities Overcoming

Extremism: the After-Charlottesville Project—a national capacity-building project, with broad bipartisan sponsorship, designed to bring state and local leaders and civil society together to share strategies for combating the rise of hate and extremist violence in our country. From the comments of those with whom I spoke after the panel, it was clear that many people had not previously understood the difference, at least under federal criminal law, between domestic terrorism and international terrorism. "International terrorism" is defined in the United States Code as activities that: (1) "involve violent acts or acts dangerous to human life," (2) violate federal or state criminal laws or would do so if committed in the jurisdiction of the United States or any state, (3) appear intended "to intimidate or coerce a civilian population," "to influence the policy of a government by intimidation of coercion," or "to affect the conduct of a government by mass destruction, assassination, or kidnapping"; and (4) "occur primarily outside the territorial jurisdiction of the United States, or transcend national boundaries." "Domestic terrorism," on the other hand, is defined in the United States Code exactly the same way, except for the fourth element. Rather than occurring primarily outside the United States or "transcend[ing] national boundaries," domestic terrorism occurs "primarily within the territorial jurisdiction of the United States."

Why then, people wanted know, are Islamist extremists who commit violent crimes in the United States with the intent to intimidate and coerce—or who merely send money or other support to Islamist extremist groups like al-Qaeda or the Islamic State—charged with crimes of international terrorism, while anti-Semites like Robert Bower and white supremacists like Dylann Roof—who killed nine black parishioners at a Charleston, South Carolina church in 2015—are charged with hate crimes but not domestic terrorism? The reason is twofold. First, for persons who commit their crimes on behalf of a designated foreign terrorist organization (FTO) like al-Qaeda or the Islamic State, those crimes are considered to "transcend national boundaries" and are thus treated as crimes of international terrorism, even if the acts that are the basis for the crimes take place in the United States. Second, although the US Code contains definitions of both international and domestic terrorism, the most commonly charged crimes of terrorism that are codified in the chapter titled "Terrorism" relate primarily to international terrorism.

For example, had the San Bernardino shooters Syed Farook and Tashfeen Malik survived their pledge of "bayat," or allegiance, to the leader of the Islamic State before using assault rifles to kill 14 people and injure many others, they likely would have faced charges for a panoply of international terrorism offenses—including providing material support to a designated FTO resulting in death and the aptly named "act of terrorism transcending national boundaries." But even though Robert Bowers committed a strikingly similar crime using an assault rifle and other firearms, there is no terrorism crime that applies to his conduct. Had he used a bomb or radiological dispersal device or nuclear material, he could have been charged with a crime included in the "Terrorism" chapter of the US Code. But use of a firearm to kill and injure is not itself a federal crime of terrorism if done with intent to intimidate or coerce in furtherance of a domestic extremist cause like white supremacy, rather than a foreign extremist cause like Islamist jihad, promoted by an FTO.

Or consider James Fields's use of his car to plow into a group of counter-demonstrators at the August 2017 Unite the Right rally in Charlottesville, Va., killing Heather Heyer and severely injuring many more. Use of a vehicle to kill or injure is not a federal crime of terrorism when done to further a domestic extremist cause. Had that same act been committed by someone who did so in the name of the Islamic State, however, with intent to intimidate and coerce, it would be prosecutable as an international terrorism offense.

Some might say that there is no need for a crime of domestic terrorism to ensure adequate punishment, and that is certainly true. As I've written previously, ample criminal statutes provide for substantial punishment for those who commit violent crimes in furtherance of domestic extremist causes. Murder is a crime in all

50 states, punishable by life imprisonment or, in some states, death; and hate crimes resulting in death, like the charges faced by Robert Bowers and James Fields and previously faced by Dylann Roof, are punishable by life imprisonment or death. But you'll never see the word "terrorism" on those indictments; a successful conviction won't include the word "terrorism"; and you generally won't hear federal prosecutors referring to the offenders as terrorists, at least not before a conviction.

Could prosecutors call an alleged offender like Robert Bowers a terrorist, even without a federal crime of domestic terrorism? Probably, but the offender might then complain to the court that use of that word, where not supported by the actual crimes with which the offender is charged, unfairly prejudices the public and the jury against him and makes it impossible to get a fair trial. That's a risk many prosecutors won't take.

There's a solution to this: enact a federal crime of domestic terrorism. Such a statute need not involve the designation of domestic terrorist organizations—a proposition that arouses legitimate fears of government abuse of authority directed toward unpopular ideologies. Instead, it could penalize the commission of specifically enumerated violent crimes such as murder, kidnaping, maiming, and assault with a dangerous weapon, when committed with one of the intents already listed in the definition of domestic terrorism: "to intimidate or coerce a civilian population," "to influence the policy of a government by intimidation of coercion," or "to affect the conduct of a government by mass destruction, assassination, or kidnapping." When committed with one of these intents, crimes of domestic terrorism, while perhaps not transcending "national" boundaries, unquestionably transcend "state" boundaries. They are not merely local crimes and they are not merely hate crimes. They are crimes of terrorism—and it's time our federal criminal code recognized it.

The creation of a federal crime of domestic terrorism would also counter the widespread but incorrect notion that the federal government does not care about domestic terrorism. Although I know from my many years at the Department of Justice that the department, and other federal agencies like the Department of Homeland Security and the Federal Bureau of Investigation, are indeed concerned about domestic terrorism, there's no question that more federal resources have been put toward fighting the threat of international terrorism since 9/11 than fighting domestic terrorism. And recent data shows that, since 9/11, domestic terrorism incidents resulting in death here in the homeland occur far more frequently than international terrorism incidents resulting in death. With enactment of a federal domestic terrorism offense would come a bigger budget and more resources for preventing attacks like the assault on the Tree of Life Synagogue.

It also would provide for better record-keeping and data analysis. Under current Justice Department guidelines, every single crime charged under the Terrorism chapter of the US Code must be coordinated and approved through the department's National Security Division. Thus, the Justice Department has perfect records of every prosecution of international terrorism. But since relatively few crimes of domestic terrorism are prosecutable under that chapter, the department lacks comprehensive data on domestic terrorism incidents around the country. Perhaps the closest data set is based on voluntary reporting of hate crimes to the FBI from state and local law enforcement agencies, which severely undercounts such crimes. Although enactment of a federal domestic terrorism offense would not entirely eliminate this reporting problem, it could not help but to improve the accuracy of the data and enable better strategies to combat the threat.

Some might worry that this would open the door to increased government surveillance at home in the name of protecting against domestic terrorists. But the surveillance techniques currently used to combat international terrorism under the Foreign Intelligence Surveillance Act are limited to the collection of foreign intelligence and cannot be used solely for the collection of domestic intelligence. The criminal authorities currently on the books—which are used to investigate criminal drug trafficking gangs, child exploitation and human trafficking, and white collar crimes—are adequate to investigate crimes of domestic terrorism without any additional authorities. To the extent that the use of these existing authorities— subpoenas, search warrants, and Title III warrants, for example— causes concern when applied to investigating domestic terrorism, that's a reasonable conversation to have. But let's not keep applying a double standard in our federal criminal code, penalizing Islamist extremist violence as terrorism but most domestic extremist violence as hate crime. The crimes Robert Bowers is alleged to have committed are crimes of terrorism, and they should be prosecuted that way.

> *"It's not clear that there's any need to pass more laws against crimes like the mass shootings in El Paso and Dayton that occurred over the weekend. Murder and related forms of mayhem are already illegal in every state."*

Making Domestic Terrorism a Crime Serves No Practical Purpose

J. D. Tuccille

In the following viewpoint J. D. Tuccille argues that there is no reason to add another law to the books by making domestic terrorism officially a crime. Such acts are already dealt with under current statutes, Tuccille believes. He notes that such a law might curtail freedom of speech and legitimate protest and points out that the US government formerly considered South Africa's Nelson Mandela a terrorist, suggesting the US government has a poor track record identifying true terrorists. Thus Tuccille takes issue with Mary McCord's call for a federal law against domestic terrorism. J. D. Tuccille is a former managing editor of Reason.com and current contributing editor. Tuccille has worked for ZDNet, the New York Daily News, *and other publications.*

As you read, consider the following questions:

1. What first amendment rights would be a concern if domestic terrorism is made a federal crime?
2. How might such a law be used against African Americans, according to the viewpoint?
3. Why does the author have little faith that the US government will apply such a law fairly and effectively?

Adding its voice to the growing chorus demanding stronger laws targeting politically motivated violence, the FBI Agents Association called on Congress to make domestic terrorism a federal crime. The members of this chorus are, to various degrees, sincere, panicked, and self-serving, but they all have something in common: they're advocating a very bad idea that's bound to threaten liberty more than it hampers terrorists.

"Domestic terrorism is a threat to the American people and our democracy," said FBIAA President Brian O'Hare in a statement. "Acts of violence intended to intimidate civilian populations or to influence or affect government policy should be prosecuted as domestic terrorism regardless of the ideology behind them. FBIAA continues to urge Congress to make domestic terrorism a federal crime. This would ensure that FBI Agents and prosecutors have the best tools to fight domestic terrorism."

Coming as it does from a labor union representing law enforcement agents who would gain another law to enforce if heeded, the statement can fairly be interpreted as an answer to the question: "Siri, what's an example of rent-seeking?"

But there are other objections to creating a new federal crime of domestic terrorism that also need to be addressed, given the real fears of many of the people making the call, and the serious concerns such a law could raise.

For starters, it's not clear that there's any need to pass more laws against crimes like the mass shootings in El Paso and Dayton that occurred over the weekend. Murder and related forms of mayhem are already illegal in every state, and there's no reason to believe that the federal government is better prepared to prosecute crimes than state and local authorities, who have long experience investigating such acts and bringing their perpetrators to trial.

Some advocates of a federal domestic terrorism statute concede this point, but still want a new law for largely symbolic value.

"To be clear, it is not that there are inadequate criminal statutes on the books," writes former Acting Assistant Attorney General for National Security Mary B. McCord, who is now with the Institute for Constitutional Advocacy and Protection at Georgetown University. "But neither state-law murder charges nor hate crime charges call what happened in Charlottesville what it was—domestic terrorism—and they fail to equate it under federal law, as it deserves to be equated, with the actions of ISIS-inspired terrorists who engage in violence in pursuit of their equally insidious goals."

McCord does acknowledge First Amendment concerns that would prevent the designation of domestic groups as terrorist organizations the way the United States government tags foreign groups. For example, even while ruling that the government could penalize assistance given to foreign groups designated as terrorist organizations, Supreme Court justices noted in 2010 that they "do not suggest that Congress could extend the same prohibition on material support at issue here to domestic organizations." But she still thinks it right to pass a law if only to put domestic terrorist acts "on the same moral plane" as those committed by largely Muslim attackers overseas.

But if we're just sending messages, it might be cheaper, and safer, to issue press releases. The feds already have a sketchy track record when it comes to investigating allegations of terrorism under existing laws.

"The United States government considered Nelson Mandela a terrorist until 2008," the American Civil Liberties Union pointed out in 2017. The organization went on to note that political protesters in Portland were being tagged as "domestic terrorists" by the Department of Homeland Security, which was then including that label in reports distributed to Fusion Centers which share information with federal, state, and local law enforcement agencies. In the absence of a specific statute against domestic terrorism, that meant little more than extra scrutiny of the sort authorized under the Patriot Act. But having your name associated with the word "terrorist" in police files comes with its own risks.

"The surveillance, labeling, and incarceration of protesters, especially Black protesters, because of their alleged criminal or terrorist activity is a well-worn trope. And while it may not surprise, it should still shock," the ACLU continued.

Not to pick on McCord here—well, not too much—but she's been a steady and specific advocate of domestic terrorism legislation. And the continued mislabeling of political protesters by law enforcement authorities for the sake of special treatment raises doubts about assurances that "to the extent that fear about possible abuses remains, any domestic terrorism statute should come with appropriate oversight requirements."

That's what she and Jason M. Blazakis, a professor at the Middlebury Institute of International Studies at Monterey, offer as a safeguard for "including domestic terrorism among the list of crimes that one is prohibited from materially supporting (such as through the stockpiling of weapons)."

That's a hell of a leap of faith to place in government agencies that have rarely, if ever, earned reputations for restraint and good judgment. Are we really supposed to believe that "appropriate oversight" by federal employees will prevent their colleagues from wrongly interpreting gun collections, stored chemicals, and random tools as material support for planned terrorist actions? These are the same federal employees who are also lobbying for domestic terrorism laws, on the rather transparent grounds that it will give them more important work to do.

Or… We could go with the admission that "it is not that there are inadequate criminal statutes on the books" and keep using existing laws as needed. By whatever name, the crimes committed by terrorists are already illegal and harshly punished. Additional laws against already criminalized activity promise to be more of a jobs program for feds than a step toward improved security, and a greater threat to our freedom than to terrorists.

> *"The staggering human toll of gun violence in the US is not just a random coincidence; it is the result of political choices."*

Gun Control Is a Political Issue

Scott Lemieux

In the following viewpoint, Scott Lemieux points out that the subject of gun control is political, whether politicians want to admit it or not. The amount and frequency of gun deaths in the United States is a result of political choices. While it is impossible to say that any one death is preventable with stricter gun laws, it is no coincidence that in countries with such laws, there are fewer gun deaths. But solving the problem is not as easy as recognizing it, the author argues. In a country where rural districts are over-represented compared to urban ones, getting the votes for significant gun control seems unlikely. According to Lemieux, the epidemic of gun violence has not been "politicized" by those on the left. It has always been a political issue. The question is, what is the United States going to do about it? Scott Lemieux is a contributing opinion writer for the Guardian, *a professor of political science at the College of Saint Rose in Albany, New York, and a blogger at Lawyers, Guns and Money.*

"Gun Control Is Political. So Is Refusing to Address the Politics of Gun Violence," by Scott Lemieux, Guardian News and Media Limited, August 26, 2015. Reprinted by permission.

As you read, consider the following questions:

1. How did Australia reduce gun violence after a mass murder?
2. What are some other policies, besides a lack of gun control, that factor into gun violence?
3. How are American urban areas both under and over policed?

After the 24-year-old television reporter Alison Parker and her 27-year-old cameraman Adam Ward were killed while on camera from a lake outside of Roanoke, Virginia on Wednesday morning, the frontrunner for the Democratic nomination, Hillary Clinton, somewhat predictably tweeted that "[w]e must act to stop gun violence, and we cannot wait any longer" and Virginia governor Terry McAuliffe called for new gun control measures in the form of background checks.

The conservative response to Democrats' anodyne reactions is even more predictable: it's wrong, they say, to "politicize" individual acts of firearm violence. But gun violence in the United States has everything to do with politics—and we should be talking more, not less, about the impact of America's failed gun policies on victims and their families and communities.

It is true—as apologists for the status quo will be sure to point out—that it is impossible to know whether today's murder specifically could have been prevented by a more stringent gun control regime, let alone by one characterized exclusively by background checks. But on a more systematic level, the result of our lack of substantive, internationally comparable gun control is entirely clear: the US is not only an international outlier in its lack of gun control, it is also a massive outlier in terms of firearm violence. The ease of access to firearms clearly causes large numbers of unnecessary deaths by homicide, suicide, and accident.

Thus, the staggering human toll of gun violence in the US is not just a random coincidence; it is the result of political choices.

Gun Control is Not the Answer

Must every tragic mass shooting bring out the shrill ignorance of "gun control" advocates?

The key fallacy of so-called gun control laws is that such laws do not in fact control guns. They simply disarm law-abiding citizens, while people bent on violence find firearms readily available.

If gun control zealots had any respect for facts, they would have discovered this long ago, because there have been too many factual studies over the years to leave any serious doubt about gun control laws being not merely futile but counterproductive.

Places and times with the strongest gun control laws have often been places and times with high murder rates. Washington, DC, is a classic example, but just one among many.

When it comes to the rate of gun ownership, that is higher in rural areas than in urban areas, but the murder rate is higher in urban areas. The rate of gun ownership is higher among whites than among blacks, but the murder rate is higher among blacks. For the country as a whole, handgun ownership doubled in the late 20th century, while the murder rate went down....

Guns are not the problem. People are the problem–including people who are determined to push gun control laws, either in ignorance of the facts or in defiance of the facts.

There is innocent ignorance and there is invincible, dogmatic and self-righteous ignorance. Every tragic mass shooting seems to bring out examples of both among gun control advocates.

"The Great Gun Control Fallacy," by Thomas Sowell, Guardian News and Media Limited, December 18, 2012.

Which policies could reduce the huge number of mass killings in the US are not a mystery: after 35 people were killed in Tasmania in 1996, Australia's conservative government enacted sweeping gun control measures. The result was that both homicides and suicides by gun were immediately and sharply reduced, and there have been no mass killings in the country since. Conversely, there have been 885 mass killings in the United States since December

2012, when a gunman killed 20 elementary school students at the Newtown Elementary School in Sandy Hook, Connecticut.

Identifying the policy changes that could reduce American firearm slaughter is easy, of course—and figuring out a politically viable way of getting these policies enacted is another matter. Even if the 2008 Supreme Court decision in *District of Columbia v Heller* declaring an individual right to bear arms in the 2nd Amendment were to be overruled by the same court, the political obstacles in the path of meaningful gun control are formidable. Isolated state and local measures aren't meaningless, but there are distinct limits to how much they can accomplish. Tough federal gun control measures could make a big difference, but passing any such measure through both the House and a Senate that massively over-represents small, rural states with a disproportionate number of gun-owners would be impossible for the foreseeable future.

The lack of congressional reaction to the Sandy Hook massacre in 2012 is instructive on that point. Even very modest, overwhelmingly popular gun control measures, involving background checks and controls on assault weapons and high-capacity magazines, failed to pass a Democratic Senate and, even if they had, they would have had no chance of passing the House of Representatives. Australian-style gun control is not coming to the US anytime soon, especially with support for gun rights only growing.

But gun control isn't the only way to address gun violence, and Parker and Ward are not even its typical victims. Even had Parker and Ward's killer not turned his gun on himself, there would have been an intensive investigation into their deaths, and the sure-to-have-been apprehended killer would have faced some measure of justice.

Consider, though, the situation 280 miles northeast of Roanoke in Baltimore, Maryland. The horrifying death of Freddie Gray in police custody has highlighted the violence committed by police against Baltimore's African-American citizens, but what the police have failed to do for the community is also important to understanding how gun violence typically plays out in America. So far in 2015, more people have been killed in Baltimore (population 620,000) than in New York City (population 8.4 million). The more than 200 murder victims in Baltimore receive much less attention from either the investigating authorities or the media, and the vast majority of those victims are poor and African-American. Indeed, the horrifying spike in homicides has been met with a weak response by the police: the clearance rate for murders is less than 40%.

A lack of federal gun control is certainly a large part of the problem of the toll of gun violence. But other policies and social conditions—most obviously high levels of economic and racial inequality—also play a major role, and both are also the result of political choices.

As the journalist Jill Leovy explains in her new book *Ghettoside*, poor African-American communities in many American urban areas are simultaneously over- and under-policed: they are on the one hand subject to routine harassment, detention, and imprisonment for minor offenses but, when it comes to serious violent offenses committed a*gainst* poor African-Americans, the reaction by the state and the media is too often apathetic or ineffectual. Most victims of gun violence will never make international news, and their deaths will almost never result in calls for more gun control—let alone the kind of gun control that would reduce the number of guns in the hands of Americans, which is the only tried-and-true method for reducing gun violence.

The American epidemic of gun violence has not been "politicized" by those who seek to alleviate it. It is and always has been an inherently a political question, as is what we're going to do about it. The answer, at least for now, seems to be "nothing". But it doesn't always have to be.

> *"Research consistently shows there is no evidence people living with mental illness are more violent than anyone else. In fact, people with mental illness are more likely to be victims of violence than other people."*

Blaming Domestic Terrorism on Mental Illness Is a Mistake

Clarke Jones

In the following viewpoint Clarke Jones argues that the link between mental health issues and mass murder is overstated: There is no evidence that those with mental health problems are more violent that the rest of society. When violence is committed by someone with mental health issues, the media tends to sensationalize it. But the majority of violent acts are committed by those without mental illness, Jones states. Instead of stigmatizing marginalized people, we should focus instead on making everyone feel welcome in society. This would go a long way toward reducing terror attacks. Clarke Jones is a research fellow at the Research School of Psychology of Australian National University.

As you read, consider the following questions:

1. Why should people stop blaming Muslims for terror attacks, according to the viewpoint?
2. What does current research say about the link between mental health and terrorist attacks?
3. What can government and media do instead of pointing fingers at those they believe are to blame?

Following another act of fatal violence in Melbourne's CBD last Friday, Prime Minister Scott Morrison dismissed claims the perpetrator, Hassan Khalif Shire Ali, had a mental illness. He said this was a "lame excuse", saying he wanted imams and the Muslim community to pay greater attention to people at risk of radicalisation.

Media reports have stated Ali suffered delusions and substance abuse problems in the lead-up to his attack and believed he was being chased by "unseen people with spears". Ali's family and religious teacher have also attested to him being mentally ill.

To be sure, most Australians will find it hard to forget the horror of this incident where three people were stabbed. Regardless of our cultural and religious backgrounds, we stand united in grieving for restaurant owner Sisto Malaspina, who was killed in the attack. But we must also try to make sense of it by analysing the perpetrator's actions and developing ways to prevent further acts of violence.

It is difficult to ignore similarities with an incident that occurred on the same street in 2017, when James Gargasoulas drove his car into a crowd of people, killing six and wounding 30. He too was said to be suffering delusions, though, interestingly this was not labelled as an excuse.

If we blame Muslim communities or cultural minorities as responsible for acts of terrorism, we are likely to continue to alienate at-risk individuals and the communities that support them. This can, in itself, lead to mental health problems. While this doesn't

Mental Illness Is Not the Cause of Domestic Terrorism

Domestic terrorism is a planned, politically-driven action. Studies have repeatedly confirmed that domestic terrorism and other violent crimes fail to be associated with mental illnesses. We must get this clear. The belief that mentally ill people are the perpetrators of domestic or international terrorism is like any other myth, only this one's particularly harmful. People with mental illnesses may be the most stigmatized group in our population. The effort to link mental illnesses to violence is adding to the burden of stigma the mentally ill carry.

People suffering from mental illness are more likely to be the VICTIMS of violent crime; they are rarely—the perpetrators of violent crime.

When terrorism is International or carried out by racial/ethnic minorities, no one has a problem seeing the action as a political crime. No one labels Muslim extremists as suffering from mental illness, even when they carry out violent actions. But when the terrorist is a white male, many influential members of the government and media and/or news influencers repeatedly promote the erroneous link between the violence and mental illness. It equates to giving the perpetrator a break; "Feel sorry for him, he has an illness."

We might want to tell ourselves that this erroneous story—this linking mental illness to domestic terrorism—is a mistake, after all anyone can make a mistake.

More likely, it's a deliberate effort to protect a White male supremacist.

We need to support people with mental illnesses, not add to the stigma they endure.

"Mental Illness Is Not the Cause of Domestic Terrorism," by Lynn E. O'Connor, PhD, Medium Corporation.

mean the result will be violence, it can increase the chances of young people dropping out of the social support system, which can lead to criminality, anti-social behaviour, self-harm or suicide.

Terrorism and Mental Illness

Research consistently shows there is no evidence people living with mental illness are more violent than anyone else. In fact, people with mental illness are more likely to be victims of violence that other people. They are also more at risk of homicide, suicide and self-harm.

It is too early to make firm conclusions about the role of mental health problems and terrorism as few studies have examined this relationship. But from these, we can establish not all terrorist incidents have mental illness as a causal factor.

A 2017 study conducted by the Combating Terrorism Centre (which was set up to understand terrorism after the September 11 attacks), analysed media reports of attackers who allegedly had a mental illness.

It found that out of 55 attacks in the West, where 76 individuals involved were possibly influenced by Islamic State, 27.6% had a history of psychological instability. This percentage is comparable to that found in the general population.

Almost half (45.5%) of Australians experience a mental health disorder at some point in the lifetime. And a 2017 survey found one in five, or 20% of the Australian population aged 16-85 years, were found to have experienced mental disorders in the previous 12 months.

The study also notes its results are not conclusive. This is because media reports are often marred by a "tendency to treat all mental health disorders equally" and a fetished way of reporting on mental illness.

Mental illness is a general term that refers to a group of disorders including anxiety, depression, bipolar disorders and schizophrenia. It can significantly affect how a person feels, thinks, behaves, and interacts with other people.

Whether or not mental illness contributes to violent behaviour is likely to differ from case to case depending on an individual's diagnosis, prior experiences, co-existence of other stressors and vulnerabilities, and lack of protective factors.

Better Support for Marginalised Communities

In the public perception, mental illness and violence often tend to be intertwined. And much of the stigma associated with mental illness may be due to a tendency to conflate mental illness with the concept of dangerousness.

This is further augmented by the media, which sensationalises violent crimes committed by people with mental illness, particularly mass shootings. The focus is often on mental illness in such reports and ignoring the fact most of the violence in society is caused by people without mental illness.

This bias contributes to the stigma faced by those with a psychiatric diagnosis, which in turn contributes to non-disclosure of the mental illness and decreased treatment seeking.

We also know that people who are unemployed, marginalised, isolated, homeless or who have been incarcerated, have significantly higher levels of mental illness than the general population. People living in socioeconomically less affluent areas have higher levels of mental illness, particularly depression.

We need culturally appropriate models of care to help with individual experiences of stigma, isolation, disengagement, and past experiences of torture and trauma.

It is not to diminish our grief and horror at last Friday's incident to tread carefully in laying blame on culture, religion, or even mental health. We know there are many reasons for acts of terrorism or violent crime. But we can minimise them by ensuring communities of all backgrounds feel part of Australian society.

Sadly, my ongoing research shows there is currently limited capacity for culturally sensitive mental health services to respond to alerts from communities about impending or actual crises. Decreasing funding and support from governments means community services are not equipped to prevent incidents like the attacks in Melbourne or manage young people of concern.

Instead of pointing the finger, perhaps governments at both state and federal levels should ask how they themselves can better support communities in dealing with the causes of violent crime.

Periodical and Internet Sources Bibliography

The following articles have been selected to supplement the diverse views presented in this chapter.

Jason Blazakis, "Domestic terrorism is fueled by paranoid delusions. Here's how we fight them." *Philadelphia Inquirer*, August 18, 2019. https://www.inquirer.com/opinion/commentary/domestic-terrorism-white-supremacy-us-government-strategy-20190818.html

Nick Blumberg, "A Conversation About Domestic Terrorism, Mental Health and Racist Rhetoric." WTTW, August 5, 2019. https://news.wttw.com/2019/08/05/conversation-about-domestic-terrorism-mental-health-and-racist-rhetoric

Lee Carter, "Gun control is what most Americans want – Here's the only way for both sides to get there." Fox News, August 9, 2019. https://www.foxnews.com/opinion/lee-carter-gun-control-is-what-most-americans-want-heres-the-only-way-for-both-sides-to-get-there

Sundiata Cha-Jua, "The horror of a new domestic terrorism law." *News-Gazette*, October 6, 2019. https://www.news-gazette.com/opinion/real-talk-the-horror-of-a-new-domestic-terrorism-law/article_04899355-ebaa-59f2-a3fe-a670c304261a.html

Debra DeAngelo, "Our problem isn't gun violence — it's domestic terrorism." Enterprise, February 24, 2018. https://www.davisenterprise.com/forum/opinion-columns/our-problem-isnt-gun-violence-its-domestic-terrorism/

"Domestic Terrorism Prevention Act of 2019." Congress. Gov, March 27, 2019. https://www.congress.gov/bill/116th-congress/senate-bill/894/text?q=%7B%22search%22%3A%5B%22white+-supremacy%22%5D%7D&r=1&s=2

"Gun Violence and Mass Shootings." Anti-Defamation League, August 2019. https://www.adl.org/education/resources/tools-and-strategies/table-talk/gun-violence-mass-shootings

Ryan Honeyman, "White People: Let's Talk About White Supremacy." LIFT Economy, October 24, 2018. https://www.lifteconomy.com/blog/2018/10/24/white-people-lets-talk-about-white-supremacy

David A. Lowe, "The tide is turning for gun control in the US." *Al Jazeera*, September 26, 2019. https://www.aljazeera.com/indepth/opinion/tide-turning-gun-control-190926093608170.html

Joe Moreno, "A domestic terrorism law is not enough to combat gun violence." Hill, August 19, 2019. https://thehill.com/opinion/national-security/457770-a-domestic-terrorism-law-is-not-enough-to-combat-gun-violence

Shirin Sinnar, "Applying 9/11 laws to domestic terrorism could hurt minorities more than white supremacists." *USA Today*, September 11, 2019. https://www.usatoday.com/story/opinion/2019/09/11/reform-9-11-terrorism-laws-dont-expand-to-white-supremacists-column/2258400001/

Clint Watts, "Countering Domestic Terrorism: Examining the Evolving Threat." Foreign Policy Research Institute, September 25, 2019. " https://www.fpri.org/article/2019/09/countering-domestic-terrorism-examining-the-evolving-threat/

Stephen N. Xenakis, "After Odessa: We need a military-scale fight against domestic terrorism and gun violence." *USA Today*, September 5, 2019. https://www.usatoday.com/story/opinion/2019/09/05/fight-gun-violence-domestic-terror-like-we-fought-islamic-state-column/2197369001/

For Further Discussion

Chapter 1

1. After reading the viewpoints in this chapter, do you believe that defining domestic terrorism is a problematic issue? What factors cause the problems?
2. How serious do you believe the threat of domestic terrorism currently is? Why? Use material from viewpoints you've read to support your argument.
3. Is white nationalism a more serious threat than other types of terrorism, including Islamic terrorism? Why or why not?
4. How does assessing the current threat of domestic terrorism become a political issue? Does your viewpoint change if you are assessing the threat from a leftist (liberal position) as opposed to a right-wing (conservative) position. Support your stance using viewpoints from this chapter.

Chapter 2

1. Do you believe that violent protests, such as those in Hong Kong, can be classified as domestic terrorism (As China has suggested)? What factors play into your answer?
2. Is domestic terrorism against innocent civilians ever justified, even if those citizens are not the targets but collateral damage?
3. Can the actions of violent anti-abortion, anti-facist, or environment groups be justified?
4. After reading the viewpoints in this chapter, do you believe that a country is capable of terrorism against its citizens or does a country have the right to deal with rebellious citizens as it sees fit to preserve itself? Why or why not?

Chapter 3

1. Do you believe that President Donald J. Trump is complicit in motivating white nationalist domestic terrorists? Why or why not?

2. Do you believe that violent video games and movies spur on domestic terrorists? Or do you believe that these are just made-up excuses? Use evidence to support your answer.

3. Should something be done about web sites and chat rooms that promote violence and stir up hate, or does the first amendment support the rights of those who attempt to radicalize people on the internet?

4. How far should the first amendment extend when it comes to freedom of speech vs. what is now called "hate speech"? Should citizens be allowed to say whatever they want in public, on the internet, and in the media without fear of condemnation or retaliation?

Chapter 4

1. Gun control is such a controversial issue in American society. Would eliminating so-called "assault weapons" limit domestic terrorism? Or do you believe other factors are more important? Why or why not?

2. How does one terrorist event often lead to another? In what ways can terrorism in which a domestic terrorist responds to an earlier attack be limited?

3. Should mental health be considered when trying to prevent domestic terrorism? Why or why not?

4. After reading the viewpoints in this chapter, do you believe the government has the right to "spy" on its own citizens to prevent domestic terrorism?

Organizations to Contact

The editors have compiled the following list of organizations concerned with the issues debated in this book. The descriptions are derived from materials provided by the organizations. All have publications or information available for interested readers. The list was compiled on the date of publication of the present volume; the information provided here may change. Be aware that many organizations take several weeks or longer to respond to inquiries, so allow as much time as possible.

American Civil Liberties Union (ACLU)

125 Broad Street
New York NY 10004-2400
(212)549-2500
email: aclu@aclu.org
website: www.aclu.org

The ACLU considers itself to be the nation's guardian of liberty, working in courts, legislatures, and communities to defend and preserve the individual rights and liberties that the Constitution and the laws of the United States guarantee. Among the issues they focus on are human rights, racial equality, and women's rights. Recent articles on their searchable website include "White Supremacist Violence Is on the Rise. Expanding the FBI's Powers Isn't the Answer," and "The Trump White House's Actions Recall the Most Divisive Eras of the American Past."

American Enterprise Institute for Public Policy Research (AEI) American Enterprise Institute

1789 Massachusetts Avenue NW
Washington, DC 20036
(202) 862-5800
email: tyler.castle@aei.org
website: www.aei.org

The American Enterprise Institute is a conservative public policy think tank that sponsors original research on the world economy,

US foreign policy and international security, and domestic political and social issues. AEI is dedicated to defending human dignity, expanding human potential, and building a freer and safer world. Their scholars and staff advance ideas rooted in their belief in democracy and free enterprise. Articles on the site include "What Makes a Terrorist," and "Antifa are domestic terrorists. Meet their academic apologist."

Anti-Defamation League (ADL)

605 Third Avenue
New York, NY 10158-3650
(212) 885-7700
website: www.adl.org

The ADL fights against all forms of bigotry and hate, and defends civil rights for all citizens. The ADL operates on the front lines, fighting anti-Semitism and hate, providing educational resources to schools, working with elected officials to strengthen hate crimes laws, and supporting communities times of need. Articles such as "A Dark & Constant Rage: 25 Years of Right-Wing Terrorism in the United States" are available as downloadable PDFs on their website. Other articles on their searchable website include "The Significance of the Oklahoma City Bombing" and "New Hate and Old: The Changing Face of American White Supremacy." They also have a fascinating pictorial database of symbols commonly used by white supremacist and other hate groups.

Cato Institute

1000 Massachusetts Avenue NW
Washington, DC 20001-5403
(202) 842-0200
website: www.cato.org

The Cato Institute is a libertarian public policy research organization, a think tank dedicated to the principles of individual liberty, limited government, free markets, and peace. Its scholars and analysts conduct independent research on a wide range of policy issues.

Articles include "Is The Domestic Terror Threat 'Overblown'? " "The Truth about Foreign-Born Domestic Terrorists," and "Homegrown Failure: Why the Domestic Terror Threat Is Overblown."

Center for American Progress

1333 H Street NW, 10th Floor
Washington, DC 20005
(202) 682-1611
website: www.americanprogress.org

The Center for American Progress is a public policy research and advocacy organization which presents a liberal viewpoint on economic and social issues. Their website includes a range of articles on various forms of terrorism and violence, including "Gun Violence in America: A State-by-State Analysis," and "Confronting the Domestic Right-Wing Terrorist Threat."

Federal Bureau of Investigation (FBI)

The FBI Headquarters
935 Pennsylvania Avenue NW
Washington, DC 20535
(202) 324-3000
website: www.fbi.gov

The FBI's mission is to protect the American people and uphold the Constitution of the United States. Their priorities include protecting the United States from terrorist attack, against foreign intelligence operations and espionage, and against cyber-based attacks and high-technology crimes. They combat public corruption at all levels, protect civil rights, combat transnational/national criminal organizations, fight major white collar crime, and combat significant violent crime. Their website contains news and articles about the fight against terrorism, in addition to their famous list of most wanted criminals.

Southern Poverty Law Center

400 Washington Avenue
Montgomery, AL 36104
(334) 956-8200
website: www.splcenter.org

The SPLC fights hate and bigotry and to seeks justice for the most vulnerable members of society. Using litigation, education, and other forms of advocacy, the SPLC works toward a time when its goals of equal justice and equal opportunity will be a reality. The website is a trove of information, and includes "Extremist Files," "Hatewatch," and numerous other resources for researching domestic terrorism. They can be contacted via a general inquiry form on their website.

US Commission on Civil Rights (USCCR)

US Commission on Civil Rights
1331 Pennsylvania Avenue NW, Suite 1150
Washington, DC 20425
(202) 376-7700
website: www.usccr.gov

Established as an independent, bipartisan, fact-finding govenment agency, the USCCR's mission is to inform the development of national civil rights policy and enhance enforcement of federal civil rights laws. They pursue this mission by studying alleged deprivations of voting rights and alleged discrimination based on race, color, religion, sex, age, disability, or national origin, or in the administration of justice. Their website contains reports such as "In the Name of Hate: Examining the Federal Government's Role in Responding to Hate Crimes," and documents including the "US Commission on Civil Rights Statement on Charlottesville, Virginia."

US Department of Homeland Security

2707 Martin Luther King Jr Avenue SE
Washington, D.C. 20528
(202) 282-8000
website: www.dhs.gov

The Department of Homeland Security has a simple yet vital mission: to secure the nation from the many threats it faces. This requires the dedication of more than 240,000 employees in jobs that range from aviation and border security to emergency response, from cybersecurity analyst to chemical facility inspector. The website includes reports such as "Department of Homeland Security Strategy for Countering Violent Extremism," which is downloadable as a PDF.

Bibliography of Books

Anita Croy. *Terrorism: Are We All at Risk?* New York, NY: Lucent Press, 2020.

P. M. Currie, Max Taylor, and Donald Holbrook. *Extreme Right Wing Political Violence and Terrorism*. New York, NY: Continuum International Publishing Group, 2013.

Eamon Doyle. *Political Extremism in the United States*. New York, NY: Greenhaven Publishing, 2019.

Michael Erbschloe. 2019. *Extremist Propaganda in Social Media: A Threat to Homeland Security*. Boca Raton, FL: CRC Press, 2019.

Martin Gitlin. *Mass Shootings*. New York, NY: Greenhaven Publishing, 2021.

Gus Martin. *Essentials Of Terrorism: Concepts and Controversies*. Thousand Oaks, California: SAGE Publications, 2019.

Terry McAuliffe and John Lewis. *Beyond Charlottesville: taking a stand against white nationalism*. New York NY: Thomas Dunne, St. Martin's Press, 2019.

Joellen McCarty. *Gun Control and the NRA*. New York, NY: Greenhaven Publishing, 2019.

George Michael. *Confronting Right Wing Extremism and Terrorism in the USA*. London, UK: Routledge, 2012.

Thomas R. Mockaitis. *Violent Extremists: Understanding the Domestic and International Terrorist Threat*. Santa Barbara, CA: Praeger, 2019.

Carla Mooney. *Domestic Terrorism*. Farmington Hills, MI: Lucent Books, 2015.

Elizabeth Schmermund. *Domestic Terrorism*. New York, NY: Greenhaven Publishing: 2017.

Andrew Silke. *Routledge handbook of terrorism and counterterrorism*. Abingdon, Oxon; New York, NY: Routledge, 2019.

Joan Smith. 2019. *Home-grown: How Domestic Violence Turns Men into Terrorists*. London, UK: Riverrun, 2019.

Donald M. Snow. *National Security*. New York, NY: Routledge, 2019.

David J. Thomas, *The State of American Policing: Psychology, Behavior, Problems, and Solutions*. Santa Barbara, CA: Praeger, 2019.

Stéfanie Von Hlatky. *Countering violent extremism and terrorism: assessing domestic and international strategies*. Montreal; Kingston; London; Chicago: McGill-Queen's University Press, 2019.

Index